A Year on Grace Street

Daily Signposts

Jeff Blake

ISBN-13: 9781981271979

For countless fellow-travelers
Who are grace in my journey
Namaste

Foreword

I first became acquainted with Jeff Blake more than forty years ago and have followed his writings in recent years.

I especially appreciate Jeff's take on radical grace and its universal access. It's a timeless message and he shares in a compelling way.

As Desmond Tutu says, "All means all" when it comes to grace. Jeff captures the thought and lives the life.

The good news is all are worthy of God's unconditional love and affirmation.

This is Jeff's focus and I heartily commend his writing.

Michael T. Christensen
Author of several books including *The Samaritan's Imperative*
Editor of the Henri Nouwen spiritual trilogy
Non Profit Founder & Director at WorldHope Corps

January 1

There is a thread that runs through our lives called grace.

This thread has no origin or end. It weaves rich textures in a tapestry that is our journey.

Sometimes we barely know this grace exists, and at other times, it overwhelms us with a depth that touches the core of our being. We get an inkling of mystery, and we are only able to whisper our gratitude.

We do not work our way into this grace, for it slips up on us, often when we are least expectant.

There is no earning this experience for it is a gift, and not one of us is denied this gift regardless of our past or present circumstance. We simply open our hands like children and accept what is given.

Grace is a resounding yes when all other voices say no. Grace comes running after us while we are yet a long way from home. Grace is the turnaround. Grace changes us from the inside out.

We are accepted just as we are—no conditional clauses, no strings attached.

The beginning of a new year is grace.

January 2

It makes no difference what we call this experience of the mind or heart. It only matters that we accept the fact that we are accepted. Not a single one of us is unimportant or unworthy, for it really has little or nothing to do with us but everything to do with a love that will not let us go.

There are a hundred ways to say grace. Grace is the chair in which we sit. Grace is an eraser. Grace is a redheaded woodpecker perched on the branch of a tree. Grace is the wings of a bird, the waves of the ocean crashing to the shore, the first coffee with a new friend, a baby's cry, a candle chasing the blues away. Grace is the evening sun that turns the trunks and roots bronze. Grace is the first magnificent light of the early morning when the earth is more still.

I wonder how you see grace and what imagination you bring to the magnificent experience of it all.

January 3

Grace Street is not Easy Street. In fact, Grace Street may be a hard row to hoe, as the old farmers say.

There may be detours, roadblocks, speed bumps, and caution or stoplights. We may get stranded alongside the road, unable to thumb a ride with a single soul. We may find ourselves on a very long stretch of barren land and feel misunderstood or isolated; particularly when it comes to building a community, but it is worth the investment if we keep going.

Every day increases our awareness that grace is our constant companion. We soar on the wings of the morning and stumble in the abyss that's hidden in the night, only to hear a voice saying, "Yes, always yes."

Always Yes!

January 4

Paul Tillich speaks of this grace: "Sometimes at that moment a wave of light breaks into our darkness and it is as though a voice were saying: 'You are accepted. *You are accepted,*' accepted by that which is greater than you, and the name of which you do not know. Do not ask for the name now; perhaps you will find it later. Do not try to do anything now; perhaps later you will do much. Do not seek for anything; do not perform anything; do not intend anything. *Simply accept the fact that you are accepted.*"

January 5

There is a profound truth about who we are and the truth is always grace.

Fyodor Dostoyevsky in *The Brothers Karamazov* -- "Above all, don't lie to yourself. The man who lies to himself and listens to his own lie comes to a point that he cannot distinguish the truth within him, or around him, and so loses all respect for himself and for others. And having no respect he ceases to love."

The truth is we are love and with each fleeting day, each passing year, we are called to love more deeply and fully than we have every loved before.

January 6

Grace woke me up this morning / grace started me on my way /
grace will help you tell your story.
—from an old spiritual

I have always had a longing for home. It seems there has been a certain sense of displacement, not quite fitting in one place or another. I can't quite put my finger on it. I only know a certain place of grace has been given along the way, if only for a little while.

I am not sure if Thomas Wolfe was right or wrong when he said, "You can't go home again."

And where is home? I take my clue from the Ninetieth Psalm. It's the psalm I asked the minister to read at both my mother and father's funerals.

God is our home. Wherever God is, we are at home and singing the songs of grace.

January 7

I am forever grateful for Frederick Buechner's incredible book *Telling Secrets.*

Buechner writes, "I have come to believe that by and large the human family all has the same secrets, which are both very telling and very important to tell. They are telling in the sense that they tell what is perhaps the central paradox of our condition—that what we hunger for perhaps more than anything else is to be known in our full humanness, and yet that is often just what we also fear more than anything else."

Grace is telling our secrets.

January 8

A couple of lines in Gershen Kaufman's book *Shame: The Power of Caring* transformed my life.

He writes, "Letting go of those troublesome, forever-to-be-unmet needs tied to those significant others who have failed us is one of the hardest of all things. For it means closing a door on the past and accepting what may be a painful reality: I cannot go back and get it the way I needed it then. Some holes will inevitably remain inside."

We close a door, accept a painful reality, and the grace of healing begins to occur. This was not a once-for-all experience; it was a daily appropriation or the acceptance of a grace which makes us whole.

Grace is closing a door and opening a new one.

January 9

Life is a long journey and our travels are always about grace.

I ran away from home metaphorically as soon as I could when I was growing up. I went off to school in Kentucky, and although Kentucky is a border state, it is not the old South. I needed the freedom to explore a new way of thinking. I knew there was a big world out there, and I was more than ready to explore it. I was, as Willie Morris put it in the title of one of his books, going north toward home.

Like many from my region of the country, I had a love/hate relationship with the South. If you read Carson McCullers's *The Heart Is a Lonely Hunter* or W. J. Cash's classic *The Mind of the South* or Ralph McGill's *The South and the Southerner* or the immortal words of Harper Lee in *To Kill a Mockingbird*, you will get a sense of what I was up against and what drove me to seek a new home.

Providential grace leads us to a brand-new world, and for the first time in our lives, the pieces of the puzzle were coming together.

January 10

There is a grace that accompanies our comings and goings, our full circles. Looking back, I count it all grace for every trial and tribulation; every mountain has been brought low and every valley exalted. There was always water in the wilderness and plenty of food at the table.

Say it again Anne Lamott, "I do not understand the mystery of grace— only that it meets us where we arc and does not leave us where it found us."

January 11

A traveler,
Let that be my name.
—Bashō

I had an old T-shirt I've been wearing around for just about twenty years. My mama gave it to me one year when she came home from a trip out West. It's a *Route 66* T-shirt, ragged, full of holes, wearing very thin in places, but I just can't part with it. It reminds me of her, and it also reminds me that, I think, wanderlust must be in my DNA.

Some people are homebodies, not me. Get me on the open road with spirits like Jack Kerouac and we'll make some dust.

They say Kerouac's book was full of the world, which is fine with me. I also think his book was his hunger for the other, maybe for God. And maybe that's what we're all after when we roam. Me? I am glad to be traveling on Grace Street with billions of other people on this earth.

January 12

Memories come tumbling into my mind: a ride on a camel to the pyramids of Egypt; a cruise on the Nile to the ruins of antiquity; the waves of the Mediterranean Sea on the island of Cyprus; the cedars of Lebanon; an unusual snowfall on a Sunday in Istanbul; the crumbling Berlin Wall; a furnace in a concentration camp where I wept; a walk across the Thames to the Globe to hear Shakespeare's work, the Great Bard's words immortalized; Westminster Abbey and the Sacrament one early morning with a handful of worshipers at St. Paul's in London; the gutted ruins of the Coventry Cathedral, north of London, where only a charred cross remains; a stroll on a summer day in Stratford-upon-Avon; the train to Edinburgh and the train from Moscow to St. Petersburg; a magnificent night in Prague; or that day on the ancient streets of Jerusalem; a prayer among the olive trees outside the Eastern Gate; a boat out on the Sea of Galilee; the Colosseum and catacombs of Rome; the Parthenon in Athens; viewing the Book of Kells in Dublin; stopping by the grave of the poet W. B. Yeats on the way to Belfast, Northern Ireland; or wandering the back roads of Scotland where the rainbows perpetually cross the sky.

Grace is exploring this great big beautiful world.

January 13

I have this insatiable thirst to see this magnificent world, to hear the voices of people in their native tongues, and to know we are one—all the people, imagine all the people. I stand on an infinitesimally small speck of ground, and I know out there is this vast, endless world. We think our space, our little dot, is all there is or all that matters when there is a universe of infinity beyond the place where we are.

Grace is seeing the vast universe and our oneness in it.

January 14

The Abbey of Gethsemani in Bardstown, Kentucky, is the one place on earth I am most deeply at home. I have been there many times, and each time, the experience is unique and different. It was here that Thomas Merton spent much of his life. He and all who seek the solitude of Gethsemani see two words— *God Alone*—chiseled above the entrance to the cloistered area.

It is the oldest Trappist monastery in the United States and the place most all the writings of Merton were created.

Right now as I write, I see a photograph above my desk of the Dalai Lama kneeling at the grave of Merton while brother monks look on from a distance.

January 15

There is an emerging interest in monastic spirituality in Protestant circles, including a high regard for the Celtic tradition, and I have greatly cherished many opportunities for personal retreats at Saint Meinrad Archabbey in southern Indiana and the Monastery of the Holy Spirit outside Atlanta.

I need quietness, solitude, and centering moments to put life in perspective and to regain a sense of the sacred. Life can easily get fractured and disjointed. Simply being still is a great need in my journey.

Someone said, "We will either go apart or we will come apart."

Grace is going apart for a while.

January 16

There is a huge ginkgo tree in the cloistered area at the Abbey of Gethsemani where Thomas Merton would often sit with seekers from around the world. I can only begin to imagine the conversations that were held on that holy ground. Looking out a window at the tree, I wrote this poem one day.

Under the Ginkgo Tree

O mercy,
mercy great,
under the ginkgo tree
where east meets west
in perfect harmony,
your branches gently covering me.
Halfway between the noisy earthbound path
and the solitude which leads to the deeper way of union.
For a hundred years and more, through seasons
of solitude, you have stood in this place by
enduring light, basking in your splendor.
I listen to your leaves as they
turn brilliantly yellow all
it seems in a day.
Falling the next
day to earth.
Under the
ginkgo
tree.

January 17

I go to the Abbey of Gethsemani for solitude, quietness; to be at home.

Years ago, I wrote this in my journal about that sacred place: "I ran slowly from your suffocating arms the first night we met many years ago. I was afraid of your silence, your otherness. For you see, I am both sons, prodigal and elder, free spirit of the wind and lost in the dead law, living in the shadows, yet so very hungry for your light.

"You there, on the crucifix. Come down. Come down. Do you remember me?"

January 18

What joy to walk through the woods to Merton's hermitage.

I sat at the wooden table where Merton wrote a number of his books.

I knelt in the little room at the hermitage where he prayed and gazed at a wooden crucifix and icons he had placed on the wall. I saw the single bed where he slept, his bookcase, his rocking chair, the fireplace where he was warmed on cold winter days. The monks had prepared for me a lovely soup with many vegetables. I broke bread and drank wine, and I knew I would never forget.

I wrote this about Gethsemani at the desk of Merton: "When the heavens were as brass, you found me. Through all darkness, you saw me. Pulling up a thousand roots, you anchored me. In this cracked earthen vessel in my altogether earthiness, you discovered me. This is my house. Your heart is my geography. Remember me. I know your name. Your name is Grace."

January 19

I took the commuter train out to Long Island, and then, I think, I took a cab to the weathered farmhouse in Huntington Station, New York, where Walt Whitman was born. It's a simple house—this place of his roots and from which he would sing his song of yes to the world and all people, becoming the great American poet.

Years later, the Delta jet landed in Philadelphia one day, and I got a rental car, drove across the river to Camden, New Jersey, and to the house where Whitman died. I saw the handwritten death notice, which was originally nailed to the door of the house, the bed where he died, a pair of his shoes, one of his hats, a couple of his rocking chairs, and remembered his words, "Your very flesh shall be a great poem."

I drove a few miles over to his grave where these words are chiseled in stone near the mausoleum where he is buried: "His life was an affirmation of freedom, His poetry a celebration of life, And his philosophy was a preparation for death."

January 20

Let us go to Luckenbach, Texas, with Waylon and Willie and the boys. I've been there several times, way out in the country, west of Austin, a place off the road with a big welcoming heart. Bikers with beards and ladies in their bikinis. Cowboys and city slickers. Ordinary folks like me. Miserable failures and folks for whom grace came running. Nothing like sitting under an old oak tree, drinking a beer or two, listening to the guitar strummers and the fiddle players, and knowing that after we stop fighting like the Hatfields and the McCoys, we're really just one family. Maybe it's time we got back to the basics of love.

Grace is getting back to the basics of love.

January 21

The Bishop's Garden at the Washington National Cathedral is a place I treasure. There on the hill, in the shadow of the great cathedral, I have sat for long hours where the fountain flows. We need our modest places of worship, but we always need great cathedrals that express the great longing we all share for the spiritual. There are always the lovely flowers of the season. There is also a sculpture of the prodigal son in his father's embrace. Not many miles away is the seat of our nation's government, and as I have sat in the garden, I have wondered what makes for peace. Maybe we grow our gardens to nurture peace within and to offer a hand of peace to the world.

January 22

Of all the monuments in the capital of our nation, my favorite is the one immortalizing Franklin Roosevelt. It's on the banks of the Tidal Basin where the cherry trees grow, in view of the Jefferson Memorial. One of my mother's wishes was to walk among the cherry blossoms one fine day in spring. I made it happen. It is a memory precious to my heart. FDR was the greatest president of the twentieth century, in my estimation. The memorial is large, spanning the terms of his presidency. I go there and remember other places that were important to FDR, places where I have also lingered, like the Little White House in Warm Springs, Georgia, and Hyde Park, north of New York City. Roosevelt led the United States through some awfully turbulent days, and his "the only thing we have to fear is fear itself " causes me to cease my fears for a little while and to live in the kind of hope Roosevelt inspired us to live. It is said that there was a plaque on the wall of the Oval Office when he was president, four words: "Let unconquerable gladness dwell."

January 23

Elegy at the Vietnam Wall

Buried in a grave wall of reflection.
A roll call of soldiers, a stony reminder.
I find my high school pal at E54 L21.
Immortalized forever.

January 24

I loved walking the streets of Florence, Italy. It is my favorite city on earth. Almost half of the great art of the world is there. I walk along the narrow streets, past the statues in the public square, along the banks of the Arno River, across the Ponte Vecchio to the Basilica di Santa Croce and view the tombs of Galileo, Dante, and Michelangelo. I visit the Uffizi, and my soul is stirred by the brushstrokes on canvas of the great artists of the centuries. My favorite painting there is Bellini's *The Lamentation*, which is the artist's rendering of Jesus who has died and is surrounded by those who love him—such profound humanity. I walk from the Doma in the center of the city to the Accademia and gaze for an hour on Michelangelo's *David* and sense the awesome mystery of a stone becoming a man.

January 25

One year, I flew from Atlanta to Rome and landed in the City of Seven Hills on Christmas Eve morning.

I rested awhile from the transatlantic flight, and just at dusk, I walked three miles to Saint Peter's Basilica as a misting rain fell on the city. Thousands of pilgrims were crowding into the square. A small brass ensemble was playing "Silent Night," and people were standing around a Nativity. It was, at once, idyllic, peaceful, and worshipful.

I had only been in that sacred place for a few minutes when, to my amazement, Pope Benedict appeared at a window inside his papal residence. He lit a single candle in the window and then left. I felt tears streaming down my face, not because I saw the pope, but because of the light that one small candle of hope offers to a darkened world.

Grace is a single candle in a dark world.

January 26

For more years than I can remember, I wanted to go to the little island in the Western Isles of Scotland, considered to be one of the most sacred places on earth—Iona, a spot where some say "the veil is thin" and where the connections with "the other" come quietly into the heart. St. Columba and his followers came here from Ireland in AD 563 and founded a monastery. Pilgrims from all over the earth have been traveling there since the seventh century. When I enter the abbey church through the west door, I sense the world of medieval Benedictine monks. It is a place of stark beauty, a place of communion, and I am more than a little blessed to spend the better part of a day and night there.

Grace is the thin places.

January 27

The class at the Maranatha Baptist Church in Plains, Georgia, where Jimmy Carter speaks on most Sundays of the year is a place of grace. It's a place I have heard him speak several times across the years.

I was in the crowd that Labor Day morning in 1976 in Warm Springs, Georgia, when Carter kicked off his presidential campaign, which ultimately took him to the White House. What a day as he stood on the porch of the home where Franklin Roosevelt sought serenity away from Washington, but I digress and return to Carter's class at Maranatha.

The aging president enters the room with a slight limp, with his only security those who protect him and his shield, the Bible. He lives by the old adage, "All that is not given is lost." He keeps pouring his life out for the world, traveling the globe as an agent of peace and reconciliation. Someday, I imagine, the fire in his belly will just burn out but not before he has traveled one more mile in the pursuit of justice in yet another troubled spot on the planet.

January 28

It was speculated that at the death of Jimmy and Rosalyn Carter they would be buried at his presidential library in Atlanta, but not long ago, they announced their intention to be buried on the grounds of the home where he had lived for so many years, right in the middle of Plains, with a population of six hundred.

He is a humble peacemaker, plainspoken with a yes as a yes and a no as a no. Always, his song is of faithfulness and grace. He says to the assembled class, "Every time you have a chance in life, stop and evaluate your life and determine what you should be doing now" and "We can form a partnership with God. That's what we're offered. Not a proud or arrogant way, but a humble way."

Former presidents are not as accessible as Jimmy Carter, but you can find him on most Sundays at his church.

You can shake the hands of Rosalyn and Jimmy Carter and have your picture taken with the Carters. You can hear this good man say, "Thank you for coming today."

January 29

I am not completely sure how my love of books got started. I remember in second grade, hearing our teacher read to us stories of the *Boxcar Children*. Those books just carried me away to another world of adventure and pure joy, but I do not remember how I moved along in reading until that day in a college class when we were having a conversation about John Steinbeck's *The Grapes of Wrath*. Something happened to me, something strangely wonderful, as we were reading the last scene in the book. Something compelling occurred, which put a hunger in my life to read books, and I have been reading ever since with an insatiable appetite. I remember standing at Steinbeck's grave in Salinas, California, and going over to Cannery Row in Monterey.

Grace is reading the great writers.

January 30

My mother was a lover of books, and maybe, that's where my thirst for books originated. I know it broke my heart when she grew so weary in her latter days and could not read. There were times when I read to her whole chapters of books over the telephone. We would laugh and cry, and we were right at home with each other in the pages of a book even though we were hundreds of miles apart.

Sadly, most people do not read—not even one book a year, surveys tell us. I wish I could think of a better word to describe how this makes me feel, like *sad* or *disturbed* or *disappointed* or something else. However, with all the respect I can muster, I say I feel pity for those who do not read. We have our gadgets and gizmos, our games, our social media, but what of the books we may choose to read as long as we have sight and then listen to on audio when we cannot see?

January 31

I believe the most important tangible gift a parent may give to children is to read every day to a child and somehow put a hunger and thirst for books in their moldable little hearts and minds. You readers know there is just something about holding a book in your hands, something about walking into a musty old bookstore and smelling the atmosphere. It is disappointing to see bookstores going out of business and libraries full of people who are not looking for books but for computers to use and video games to take home.

I have read hundreds of books and keep a stack on my bedside table. One of the best questions we can ask a fellow traveler is "What are you reading right now?" I enjoy reading a book while out walking; sometimes though I have to try to watch myself so as not to run into something in my way. Pat Conroy's *My Reading Life* is about the best book I have read on the life-changing power of reading.

God answers the mess of life
with one word:
'grace."

Max Lucado

February 1

Emily Dickinson said, "There is no frigate like a book to take us to that merry land," and Cynthia Tucker, former editor of the Atlanta paper wrote, "Good books liberate us from our common folly: believing we have all the answers." The longer I live, the less I know but the hungrier I am to know more.

May I suggest we think about the books that have been most important in our journeys? You may even wish to make a list of the books that have mattered in your life.

February 2

Ten most important books in my life in no particular order:

John Steinbeck's *The Grapes of Wrath*
E. Stanley Jones's *The Divine Yes*
Thomas Merton's seven-volume journals
Wendell Berry's *Collected Poems*
Flannery O'Connor's *The Complete Stories*
Parker Palmer's *A Hidden Wholeness*
Henri Nouwen's *Reaching Out*
Harper Lee's *To Kill a Mockingbird*
Michael J. Christensen's *The Samaritan's Imperative*
A Testament of Hope: The Essential Writings and Speeches of Martin Luther King, Jr.

I wonder which books have been your constant companions and have meant the most in your journey?

February 3

To Kill a Mockingbird is one of the greatest books ever written. It is one of the great social commentaries of all time.

I can't forget hearing Atticus say as he looks into Jim's eyes, "It is a sin to kill a mockingbird."

I will always remember Atticus saying, "Before I can live with other folks, I've got to live with myself. The one thing that doesn't abide by majority rule is a person's conscience."

February 4

I can hear Flannery O'Connor saying, "Don't expect faith to clear things up for you. It is trust—not certainty." I've been to the house in Savannah where she was born, to the little Catholic church in Milledgeville, Georgia, where she took the Sacrament most every day, to the farm called Andalusia where she wrote most of all her books, and to her grave beside the graves of her mother and father.

Flannery creates these characters, grotesque characters in some ways. They are misfits and freaks: a hitchhiker who kills a bickering family and the woman who marries off her mentally challenged daughter to a one-armed tramp. There's a hypocritical Bible salesman who meets a woman who has been crippled by a hunting accident, and then he seduces her and steals her wooden leg. Now just where did all that come from in Flannery's imagination?

When she was asked why she chose to write the way she did, she said, "To the hard of hearing, you shout, and for the almost blind, you draw large and startling figures."

February 5

Flannery O'Connor wrote in one of her letters: "What people don't realize is how much religion costs. They think faith is a big electric blanket, when of course it is the cross. It is much harder to believe than not to believe. If you feel you can't believe, you must at least do this: keep an open mind. Keep it open toward faith, keep wanting it, keep asking for it, and leave the rest to God."

Grace is realizing the cost of believing and living.

February 6

I have built my journey around Henri Nouwen's stages of spiritual formation from his book *Reaching Out* -- (1) loneliness to solitude, (2) hostility to hospitality, and (3) illusion to prayer. For a long time, I thought the big issue for me was loneliness to solitude, but I have discovered my place to dig deeper, and change is from hostility to hospitality. I'm known for my hospitality, but sometimes, it is less than I would like it to be.

February 7

Henri Nouwen's *The Wounded Healer* is a classic writing in spirituality. Nouwen understood the well-known Australian Aboriginal activists quote, "If you have come to help me, you are wasting your time. But if you have come because your liberation is bound up with mine, then let us work together."
Grace is understanding our oneness with all people.

February 8

I remember how Parker Palmer pulled me from a several-month pit of depression with his *A Hidden Wholeness*.

He told me not to run from the darkness but to run into it, embrace it. He taught me to live with the questions without having to have all the answers.

He wrote that his therapist said to him, "Parker, could you think of your depression as a friend trying to press you down to ground on which it is safe to stand?"

I remember having breakfast with his wife and him at Pendle Hill, the Quaker retreat center outside of Philadelphia, and telling him just how much his writings mean to me.

February 9

.

The thunderous voice of Martin Luther King is burned in my soul with his essential writings, and I will not forget that he was, first and always, a man of nonviolence, a lover of Gandhi, and a gospel preacher. I believe, every great social reform is born when we get to the authenticity of a spirituality that calls us to love God and neighbor.

Grace comes to us in the form of people like Martin Luther King.

February 10

In a naysaying world, I see E. Stanley Jones rise up after a paralyzing stroke and write about the divine yes and the yes we say to whatever comes our way. My spirit resonates with his thought of an unshakable kingdom and an unchanging person.

Grace is a resounding Yes!

February 11

I am moved by the words of Vincent van Gogh I saw on the wall of a bookstore one day, but I can't remember where. Only his words I remember: "I think that I still have it in my heart someday to paint a Bookstore with front yellow and pink in the evening . . . like a light in the midst of the darkness."

Books are lights in the darkness. They are parts of the grace that keeps us alive.

February 12

Seek not to follow in the footsteps of the men of old, rather, seek what they sought.
—Gautama Buddha

People of grace come in all shapes and sizes, all colors, all persuasions, for as we have been saying, there is a thread of grace that runs through the lives of billions of people who live on planet Earth. We may not speak the same language, but we do experience the same grace. How enriching it is to learn of the grace of another, a sojourner on whatever path we take.

I am thoroughly delighted when someone agrees to a conversation, for every single one of us has a story. I call someone up or write a letter, sometimes with fear and trembling, and I wait. I've waited a year or more in some instances, and by golly, in most instances, I get a positive response: "Sure, come to see me, let's talk," and occasionally, like with Wendell Berry, "I hope you'll come back for another conversation real soon."

February 13

Clara—Clara Phillips of Kerrville, Texas. Now there was a woman after my own heart. "You are coming to my one hundredth birthday party, aren't you?" she questioned. "Of course, Ms. Clara, I wouldn't miss it for the world." "Well then," she said, "I want you to sit right beside me at the head table." And of course, I was more than a little delighted to say yes.

Clara grew up in the mountains of Appalachia, a coal miner's daughter whose family was broken up when she was fifteen years old. She lived quite a life, recollecting most of the twentieth century. I could not begin to tell you all I learned as I sat at her feet.

She said to me quite plainly, "Your relationships with people are more important than job or money. I can say this with authority after my very long life. I never feel alone, and I am as happy as a big sunflower, and I spread it around to help make others feel good."

February 14

Clara lived in a modular home and cut her own hair so she would have more money to help others. Her considerable estate went to help young people get an education. There may be no finer way to leave a legacy. People told her she should buy things for herself, and she would only laugh and say, "I have no need for things, I only want to love."

About a month before her one hundredth birthday, she called me and said, "You know, I am just about blind, but you know what I've decided? If I am blind, I am blind, but I will keep on in all the light I'm given."

At her birthday celebration, a throng of people showed up. She whispered in my ear, "This big crowd of people, they're just hungry to be loved" and "People don't need gifts. They need to be loved."

Clara taught me by way of the grace of longevity and how life is to be lived for others. Grace is always about being and ultimately about doing.

February 15

Then there was Ralph Hammond, a man I affectionately called the Old Poet of Alabama. He lived into his ninety-fifth year. We shared a friendship around literature. We spent countless hours in delightful conversation. We talked on the telephone most every day and got together a few times a year. 47

He was the author of forty books, the poet laureate of our state, an expert on Van Gogh with over 150 books in his library on the great painter. He met and wrote about his personal encounters with Robert Frost, Pablo Picasso, Ernest Hemingway, and T. S. Eliot. He was a lifelong friend of Harper Lee and showed me their correspondence through the years.

He said, "I write simply for the joy of writing: to gladden the presence of another day, to leave a legacy of having been alive earth side, and to honor the absolute wonder of being alive."

February 16

Ralph told me one day, "When my life comes to an end, I don't have to worry about it. I just want to be doing something for others." And then he reflected in a quieter voice, "I have been accenting others more these days."

He was always "accenting others." I remember how he was influential in getting the sentence of a man on Alabama's death row changed to life. When the man was dying of natural causes in prison, Ralph knew his friend had no family, except some kin in Illinois, and thus, no place to be buried. Ralph asked the man if he wanted to be buried in the Old Poet's family plot, and if you go to the country cemetery today, you will see the graves of Ralph, Ralph's wife, and Tom Wilson, who was laid to rest there some years back.

During the last couple of years of his life, he never missed an opportunity to tell me he loved me and the difference I made in his life. "Ah, Ralph," I would say, "you're the one who is a blessing."

February 17

When Ralph was very old and coming near the end of his earthly walk and could barely move at all, he blew me away with these words: "I am going down this road with you. I will walk with you every step of the way."

Now tell me, what kind of awesome friendship is that?

Ralph's son told me he spent the last sweet night of Ralph's life with him in the hospital and that they said all they needed to say to each other. Just before he died, Ralph whispered, "Close the books."

Ralph Hammond taught me the grace of the way we care for "the least of these."

February 18

Mattie Powell lived into her ninety-fifth year. She was my beloved mentor through the years. She called me her boy, her son, and I loved every moment of it. The fact was, she had many sons and daughters whom she loved. Her heart was very tender; in fact, tears were always falling from her eyes as grace to me. I called her a weeping priest and prophet.

One of her sons was Ray Powell, and he wanted to be part of the Selma to Montgomery march in 1963. He told her that he was afraid, and she said, "We all are, son," and he asked her what he should do about marching. She just said, "Follow your heart, son," and that was more than enough to set him on his course.

February 19

Mattie and I had grand times together. She was the greatest storyteller I ever knew. I sat at her table on many occasions and enjoyed the finest Southern food imaginable. I remember a day of deep brokenness in my life when she wept with me and loved me like the mother she always was.

When she was eighty, I called her on her birthday to wish her a happy day and asked how she would be spending her day. She laughed and said she was on her way to the old folks' home to see if she could "brighten the day of some old soul who needed a little sunshine."

When she was a very old woman, I went to see her in a home for seniors. I screamed, "Ms. Mattie! Ms. Mattie! Do you know who I am?" and she screamed back, "Of course, I know who you are. Do you think I'm crazy?" We laughed till we could laugh no longer in that moment of levity near the end of her journey.

February 20

Every Easter Sunday for more than thirty years, I would call Mattie up on the phone, and she would answer with a bold and joyful "Christ is risen!" and I would respond, "Christ is risen indeed!"

She understood precisely what Wendell Berry meant when he wrote, "Practice resurrection."

She taught me the grace of resurrection, not so much in terms of a particular spiritual tradition, but of authentic living in the now.

February 21

I cannot do justice to Will Campbell with my words or tell you all I felt when I visited him at his old home outside of Nashville.

There was not a speck of phony piety in him, for he was a straight talker, and what you saw was what you got. He was an unassuming man with no pretense. He was a man of good humor, with a shaker full of salty language to flavor his stories, as well as a lover of whiskey and all people.

Grace is meeting people who make a difference in our world.

February 22

Will Campbell was one of four people who escorted the Little Rock Nine when Little Rock Central High School was integrated. He told me, "I didn't have sense enough to be scared." He was fired from the chaplaincy at the University of Mississippi and got death threats because he played ping-pong with a black man. He marched from Selma to Montgomery, was part of the boycotts and sit-ins in the South. He shared a jail cell more than once with Martin Luther King. He told me, King and he had an ongoing litany: "Will, I'm praying for you" and the response, "Martin, I'm praying for you" and King's response, "Will, we'll see who can out pray the other."

Bill Clinton presented Campbell with the National Medal for the Humanities at the White House. The medal was on the old kitchen table on the day I visited Campbell.

February 23

Ask Jimmy Carter what he thought of his friend Will Campbell, or read what Carter wrote in the foreword to Will's finest book *Brother to a Dragonfly*. It is an immensely wonderful narrative of growing up in the South during the Great Depression and especially about Will's brother Joe. He inscribed his book to me with these words: "For Jeff / Brother too / Hope / Will Campbell."

I pulled out the copious notes I have on the things he said to me during several hours of conversation. In fact, he got a telephone call while I was there and said to someone, "There's a man here who has asked me a million questions."

Grace is asking a million questions.

February 24

Oh, the stories he told me about his friendship with Thomas Merton, the funniest of which was one about sitting on the banks of the pond at the Abbey of Gethsemani and drinking beer and a little Kentucky bourbon.

On war, Campbell wrote: "Why can there not be a one-sentence peace treaty: 'It shall be a violation of international law for any nation to kill a child of another nation.' What nation would not sign the treaty? And how would war then be waged?"

On religion, he wrote: "Today we are bombarded with a theology of certitude. I don't find much biblical support for the stance of 'God told me and I'm telling you and if you don't believe as I do, you're doomed.' A sort of 'My God can whip your god's posture.'"

February 25

Those hours I spent with Will Campbell are forever burned and cherished in my memory. We sat at his kitchen table and on his back porch, walked his property, and went over to the little cabin where he wrote.

In the cabin, there were pictures of his family, including a picture of his grandmother he had written about in *Brother to a Dragonfly*. I asked him, "Is this your grandmother Bettye who got a new bathrobe for Christmas one year and thought it was so pretty that she wore it to church?" He laughed and said, "That's the one."

Somewhere along the way, he suggested I go someday to the little place in Southwest Mississippi where his family is buried in the East Fork Cemetery. "You'll find all the Campbells buried there" and "When I die, I am going to be cremated and have some of my ashes scattered over my brother Joe's grave. Who knows what he will say? Maybe 'Come on, Will. I'm glad you're here,' or maybe he'll say, 'I'm surprised as hell you made it.'"

Will Campbell loved bells. In fact, he had a habit of ringing a bell every day. I imagine it had something to do with the hope within him.

I think I'll look for a bell to ring today just for Will Campbell, just for hope.

February 26

Samuel Menashe gave me the gift of his time, which is always a gift of grace for the journey.

He was the first poet honored with the Neglected Masters Award given by *Poetry* magazine and the Poetry Foundation. He was not a well-known poet, but I hardly think popularity mattered to him. I think he wrote for the love of writing.

Menashe was essentially a religious poet though without an orthodox creed. He was a Jewish fellow who lived in a small New York apartment for almost fifty years. He died in his sleep in 2011. His poems were short, every word counted. He wrote:

> Pity us
> by the sea
> on the sands
> so briefly.

February 27

On a splendid Saturday, he signed one of his books for me and said, "Ah! I've been writing a new poem, which I think, I will share with you. Let me think. Here's how it goes."

He began to write his poem-in-the-making on a blank page at the end of his book he had already signed. With his young heart and old hand, he wrote:

Railroad Flat

Looking at the sky
From my window seat
I am in a train
Sidetracked here—
Here a lifetime—
How could I know
What day was mine
To seize, let go
Where to draw the line
Between yes and no.

Yes to Samuel Menashe and so many other poets who have poured multiple blessings into my life.

February 28

There was that day with Franz Wright.

He said, "Meet me in the public square in Waltham (Massachusetts) under the flags at the corner of Main and Moody at one-thirty."

I had time to kill, so I walked across the Charles River on a bright summer day and discovered, to my delight, a bookstore filled with used and new books. There's just something about the smell of an old bookstore.

The keeper of the store was a young man from California who told me he was a student at Brandeis, an English major. He's Jewish. He wore a *kiap*. "Partly tradition, partly respect for God," he said. Our conversation flowed naturally over literature and writers and religion. I wished I could stay all day, but it was time to meet Franz Wright.

February 29

Franz Wright walked up just before the appointed hour. He's the winner of the Pulitzer for his book of poetry *Walking to Martha's Vineyard*. He's the son of James Wright who also won the Pulitzer for poetry, the only father/son to ever win this esteemed award. He suggested, "Let's ride over to Concord for lunch and walk at Walden Pond."

Here is a man who has journeyed across the thin crust of hell, a shattered man with addictions. He's been in sobriety for a number of years. His life in the shadows of loneliness and desperation has given way to hope, a sense of meaning. I do not think it is accidental that grace often comes to us through people who have been broken.

He said he was not alone anymore. He joined the Roman Catholic Church, enduring the ridicule of several of his high-minded friends who said, "You can't believe in God and be an intellectual. Poppycock."

March 1

I drive along Route 4 West in New Hampshire to meet Donald Hall. The scenery is rural, tranquil, the quintessential geography for a poet. It's a quiet early morning, and I am on my way to Eagle Pond, the ancestral home and farm of Mr. Hall.

He tells me in advance, "My house is just beyond the Wilmot town sign. I am pretty much into solitude now, but you can come for a visit." My heart skips a beat with excitement.

We settle easily and comfortably and readily into conversation. "Mind if I ask a few questions, Mr. Hall?" "No, of course not," he demurs.

"How did you feel when you got the news of your selection as United States Poet Laureate?"

He laughs. "Pleased and surprised and then the publicity started, and I was astonished. There were two days of nonstop telephone interviews, and then the mail started, and there were over four hundred letters in just two or three days."

March 2

I say, "I understand Eagle Pond is where your roots are, where your family has lived for generations."

"Yes, Eagle Pond is my connection with history, with family, with the planet. I prize connections. I can sit by this window and look out to the mountain the same way my ancestors have looked out this window and up to the mountain."

I ask him about his spiritual journey. He says, "I don't have a body of faith. I am a Christian by choice and habit."

"What about some advice for wannabe poets?"

He says, "Read English literature and not just contemporary poets. Be acquainted with the seventeenth century, the greatest century in literature, in my opinion. Find your loves, whoever they are. Know history."

Regarding his writing style, he says, "I don't write poems. I revise them. I keep them for two years and more before I send them to a publisher. Not days or weeks but months and years I write a poem."

He intones, "It's about losing yourself in what is in front of you. I do it with writing."

We talk of fear, and he says, "Fear is fear of loss and losses, and it is intricate in human life. We lose others, we lose ourselves. I am dealing with the phenomena of old age. There is loss, emptiness around us."

March 3

Donald Hall continues, "I was an only child and didn't have many friends. I spent most of my time alone. I wrote. I love solitude."

"Have you been successful, Mr. Hall?"

"I suppose, objectively, I have been successful. I don't sit around and think about it. I think about today and tomorrow."

And he says, "I hope for what I may write" and "When you set pen to paper, you invoke hope."

"Why so many great poets from New England?"

He reflects, "Connection with the past by way of place, I'd say."

I ask, "Could you give me directions to your wife, Jane Kenyon's grave?" and he tells me what road to follow and says, "I hope you will go by there. I'll be buried beside her."

With a twinkle in his eye, he says, "The only thing remaining is the year of my death on the gravestone."

I say, "Thank you, Mr. Hall. You cannot imagine how much this visit means to me."

I find Jane Kenyon's grave, black granite stone with her name and Donald Hall's name side by side with these words chiseled into the marker: "I Believe In The Miracles Of Art But What Prodigy Will Keep You Safe Beside Me."

March 4

Jane Kenyon is probably my favorite poet. I read her *Let Evening Come* every night as a kind of surrender, a way of letting go of the day and welcoming the night. I share her poem with you:

Let Evening Come

Let the light of late afternoon
shine through chinks in the barn, moving
up the bales as the sun moves down.
Let the cricket take up chafing
as a woman takes up her needles
and her yarn. Let evening come.
Let dew collect on the hoe abandoned
in long grass. Let the stars appear
and the moon disclose her silver horn.

Let the fox go back to its sandy den.
Let the wind die down. Let the shed
go black inside. Let evening come.
To the bottle in the ditch, to the scoop
in the oats, to air in the lung
let evening come.
Let it come, as it will, and don't
be afraid. God does not leave us
comfortless, so let evening come.

On the ground at the grave below Donald Hall's name is a small stone with one word inscribed: *Hope.*

March 5

It has been Wendell Berry, the man and his writings, who has most profoundly influenced my life. It's those visits with him at his farm in Port Royal, Kentucky, to which I return in my memory now.

On the day of a visit with Wendell Berry, I had a little time to kill. I met a woman in the Port Royal Community Cemetery and asked her if she knew the writer. "Well, I've never met the man, but I hear he goes to the woods for his religion. You know, he meditates."

With those words, I began my first three-hour visit with Wendell Berry.

Berry and his wife, Tanya, live in a modest white frame house on a hill within sight of the Kentucky River where they grow a big garden in the summer and raise sheep today. He has mules for tilling the soil. He has no computer. He has written more than forty books, all in longhand.

He extended gracious Southern hospitality, laughed heartily, expressed concern for our country and the political bent to the right, decried what was happening in higher education today, and very patiently allowed me to take many pictures. He asked, "How many pictures are you going to take of me?" and I retorted, "Till I get one great one." I got a great one.

March 6

Wendell Berry and I talked about his discipline of writing, how words came to him, his first love poems written when he was in high school, his ancestors, the value of work.

I asked him if he thought much about his mortality. "Every day," he said. "I've lost most of my family and friends, my oldest literary friends are gone."

He spends a great deal of his time answering correspondence. He said, "My life consists of started conversations."

He bore down on his belief: "There's something we are all born to do—a calling, a vocation."

He said, "An artist is not a special person. Every person is an artist."

I asked him what he had learned about grace over the years. He said with a quiet detachment, "I don't know much about grace. I've experienced grace coming from somewhere beyond me."

March 7

Berry and I spoke of what I consider to be his greatest poem, "The Peace of Wild Things," and his last line, "I rest in the grace of the world and am free." It is the land he loves, all creatures great and small. I could not help but think of Thoreau and his words about nature as "an unroofed church, a place of reverence."

As I have often done in conversations with people, I asked him to speak a little about that John Donne elegy: "Pregnant again with the old twins, fear and hope." (It's a great conversation starter if you want to dig a little deeper.)

Berry said, "Well, there is plenty to be afraid of. Plenty."

He spoke of fear, particularly the fear we have, not so much of God anymore, but of ourselves in an age of "all these elegant sciences, which are getting us into fixes we can't get ourselves out of, like nuclear stock piles and nerve gas storage."

He said, "We are suffering from ourselves," and he talked of his long-standing advocacy of "leadership from the bottom" or people who saw things to do and did them, like farmers and farmers' markets. "If you want to preserve democracy," he implored, "shop at a farmers' market."

Then he spoke of hope: "There is also plenty to be hopeful about." And we talked most of pockets of thought and community life where people are living simply, learning about sustainability, and creating ways to find a way forward.

March 8

I went to Washington when Wendell Berry was honored by the country with the National Endowment for the Arts award. He was in rare form at the Kennedy Center. I also heard him say at the National Cathedral, "I am a lowlife. It's the lowlife closest to the ground where I want to live" and "I've been a student all my life. I'm still making mistakes. I am an amateur. The public thing I most value is conversation. It is the opposite of violence."

He was asked at the cathedral what character from the Bible he would like to invite to his home for a meal and what question he would pose. After a long hesitation, Berry answered, "I'd invite Simon Peter for dinner. He made a lot of mistakes. I'd ask him, 'Was all that stuff really true?'"

March 9

I remember being in a gay bar in Atlanta a few years ago. It was a place where, on Sunday afternoons, gay men got together for a drink or two and they did a rather unusual thing. They wandered off the streets to sing the old hymns of the church, songs from their past. I would hold a vodka martini in my hand and sing a gospel song that was embedded in my soul at the same time.

As we would sing, I imagined the stories of the brothers around me, their struggles with who they were. I suspected some of their stories were about the rejection of family, of churches. I imagined some of those weary travelers had just about given up on hope and yet were hanging on for a better day. I thought about those people I had known who lived through needless shame and the stigma attached to their sexual identity. I thought about how people persevere against injustice and bigotry and how we can never rest until the whole human family is free.

I heard those good men singing in that bar. I heard my own weak voice singing along with them the old spiritual, "Farther along, we'll know about it. Farther along, we'll understand why. Cheer up, my brother, live in the sunshine. We'll understand it. All by and by."

March 10

When I lived for a while in Richmond, Virginia, I would often walk in the historic Hollywood Cemetery, a sprawling cemetery characterized by rolling hills and winding paths overlooking the James River.

I actually love to walk in cemeteries, especially when I am taking life a bit too seriously and when I need to be reminded that "this too shall pass." Cemeteries remind me not to take life too seriously. They read like a book and have a history all their own. They tell us never to be forgotten stories.

This particular cemetery in Richmond is the resting place of two United States presidents, James Monroe and John Tyler, as well as the only Confederate States president, Jefferson Davis. Twenty-five Confederate generals are buried here, including George Pickett and J. E. B. Stuart, gallant men of the Civil War. I was a history major in college, so I was captivated by all my discoveries there but not because of any of these memorials, rather for a statue I came upon one day of an angel with a broken wing.

I took photographs of the broken-winged angel from all angles. I took friends of mine whom I knew were having a rough go of it to see the angel. I went there alone to ask for healing in the solitude of my own broken moments.

March 11

I remember a day in Oxford, Mississippi, when I spent some time with Neil White who wrote *In the Sanctuary of Outcasts*. Neil committed a white-collar crime and was incarcerated as an inmate at a federal prison in Carville, Louisiana, in the same community alongside people living with leprosy. He had to leave his wife and small children to serve his time.

White writes a moving true story of his life with fellow inmates as well as people who lived at the leprosarium. Their stories will tear your heart out and get your feet moving to help others.

He offered me some mighty good advice. He said, "Live simply, hide nothing, and help others." Now there's a mouthful and just might be a good solution to the complexities we get ourselves into from time to time.

But I will tell you now the most important thing he said to me. He said, "The people I want to spend my life with are the people covered with scars." Grace is not given to us to store in a bottle and tuck away on a dusty shelf, but we are called to break the bottle and share the healing salve.

March 12

Got any scars? Broken places? Sure you do if you are like me. Who do you want to spend your life with as your journey continues? Isn't there a hallelujah, albeit a broken hallelujah, as Leonard Cohen would say, that we can sing along with one another to lighten the load as we travel on Grace Street?

Fifty years ago, I got a letter from a friend that I have held on to all these years. The letter reads in part:

"Sometimes you'll wonder if the task is too much or maybe you'll wonder if you are doing any good. Then you'll look back and receive your blessings from a smile that comes on a child's face or a tear that you were able to wipe away not by being asked at the end of life how much money did you make or what big thing did you do to make a name for yourself; but was the world left a better place by you being a friend to mankind."

March 13

There's a story out of the life of Leslie Weatherhead I've been carrying around for years. When the Nazis were raining terror down on old England and Weatherhead's own church was gutted by the bombers, he wrote these words out of his own burning heart:

"When I am hot and rebellious, bitter and cynical and sarcastic, when it seems that evil can win in the world and the battle is to the strong, when it seems as though pride possesses all the high places and greatness belongs to those who can grab the most, when it seems that faith is mocked and humility is trodden in the dust, when pity seems weakness and sympathy folly, when a foul egotism rises up within me bidding me assert myself, serve my own interest and look out for number one, then, O my God, as I listen down the corridor of the years for the voice of the Almighty, may I hear the gentle splashing of water in a basin, and see the Son of God washing his disciples' feet."

March 14

Foot washers, that's what we are, spending our time with people covered with scars. We are those wounded healers with a broken wing when the awful grace of God comes to us just when we imagine there is no hope, no exit, no way forward. As Karl Barth said, "Grace must find expression in life, otherwise it is not grace."

We are those, if we listen long enough, who will hear the gentle splashing of water in a basin.

March 15

*And he got up and came to his father. But while he was still a
long way off, his father saw him, and felt compassion for him,
and ran and embraced him, and kissed him.*
                                                        —Luke 15:20

The story of the prodigal son in the fifteenth chapter of Luke
is my favorite story in the Bible because I see a father running
down a dusty road, long before the son makes it home, to
embrace and kiss his son. What a tender moment of intimacy,
which means the story may be more about the father than his
son.

I think I have always been drawn to the narrative, and
maybe, it is the underlying reason for this memoir. I know the
pull of the story has something to do with my relationship with
my own earthly father.

The story from Luke is the classic parable of grace, and there
are not many stories in my tradition that speak to me with greater
clarity. I am the prodigal, I am the father, and I am the elder
brother—all three characters in the story. Maybe you see one of
the characters or all three of the characters as who you are.
We're all there. Every one of us regardless of whether we
believe or choose not to believe. We're all the beloved.

March 16

I know what it is to be a prodigal, estranged and living among the swine, away from home. I know how it is to be the elder brother. I've wanted what I thought was mine, but what actually belongs to me? Not much. Not much of anything, really. All I think I have is a gift on loan for a little while as I walk on Grace Street with all people, *all* meaning all, which is to say, I walk alongside the whole human family, and there are no differences in any of us ultimately. The greatest lesson I learned many years ago in college is that we are pretty much all the same. Yes, we have our unique DNA, our individuality, but we share the same grace, which is what matters.

Grace is our common denominator. Grace makes us one. How futile, how foolish our attempts to divide ourselves into camps, to build walls and not bridges. We build whole philosophies, whole cultures, and whole religious systems to make sure we separate ourselves from one another. And yet in all our confusion, all our striving to run from each, there is this immense possibility to extend grace to one another. We can embrace one another, all of us, at the deepest level of our being.

March 17

This story of the Prodigal Son is ultimately about the father, and please change *father* to *mother* if it helps you on your journey. Only know that we have here the personification of grace just as our very existence is the embodiment of grace. The air we breathe, every beating second of our hearts are all grace. There is nothing for us to boast about or to make us proud or haughty or pretentious or hollow men and women stuffed with straw. There is nothing that says we're in control or ever will be. Ours is only to whisper even the faintest yes, to surrender, and to hold out our empty hands in receptivity. C. S. Lewis said, "A man whose hands are full of parcels cannot receive a gift." Why don't we just offer up our empty hands?

I heard Maya Angelou say at the first Clinton presidential inaugural in her majestic poem "On the Pulse of Morning": "Each of you, descendant of some passed-on traveler, has been paid for."

E. Stanley Jones said it best a long time ago. We can celebrate self, deny self, or we can surrender self into the loving arms of the grace, which calls us simply to be the children we always were.

March 18

That's what the story in the Bible is about—a grace that keeps wooing us, calling us to come to our senses, to remember at the core of our being, we are the beloved and we always will be. Nothing can separate us from this grace. Not trial or tribulation or circumstance, not the profound loneliness of our time, not our hostilities or illusions. It's grace. All grace.

Here's a father or mother who doesn't wait for a prodigal son or daughter to knock on the door. Here's a never-wavering, unconditional, unbreakable commitment. It doesn't get much better than this. It doesn't get any better than grace that comes running after us and kneels down in the dirt with us to pick us up just wherever we are on the way home.

P. T. Forsyth thunders home the truth: "The feeble gospel [good news] preaches, 'God is ready to forgive'; the mighty gospel preaches, 'God has redeemed.'"

I take that to mean we are already back home, the whole universe in fact.

March 19

Not in any of this writing have I intended to minimize the fact that acts are the ultimate tests of our appropriation of grace. I have intentionally placed emphasis on the pure nature of grace, which is unconditional, but as Dietrich Bonhoeffer says, there is no cheap grace. There is costliness in grace, and it always has to do with the way we treat all our neighbors, *all* meaning all as Desmond Tutu would say.

Traveling on Grace Street is a creative dualism, sometimes a conflict, a synthesizing of being and doing. Some days, we bask in grace, all grace. Some days, we roll up our sleeves and get to work. I like to imagine when the prodigal came home; he spent the rest of his life in gratitude, in living out the grace his father showed him.

March 20

If I could get on an airplane today and fly anywhere in the world that I would like to go, I would travel from Atlanta to Saint Petersburg, Russia.

I would take a cab from the airport to the State Hermitage Museum to spend as many hours as I could, observing Rembrandt's masterpiece, *The Return of the Prodigal Son*.

Art historian Kenneth Clark says of the piece that those who have seen the work "may be forgiven for claiming it as the greatest picture ever painted."

I was in the historic city of Leningrad, now Saint Petersburg, some forty-five years ago when I was growing up, but I only remember seeing the famous palace in the city. If, by some chance, I saw Rembrandt's work, I do not remember it, and maybe, it would have made little impression on me at the time. Now it would—after all these years of struggling with grace and ultimately surrendering to grace, the painting would make a profound difference.

March 21

The characters in Rembrandt's painting are all too familiar. A welcoming father, a wandering son, an older brother in the shadows, and to the right of the father and son are Rembrandt's representations of those who are so caught up in rules and law that they cannot comprehend the nature of grace shown to the wayward son. Or maybe Rembrandt is saying the truth is beginning to dawn in their cold, stony hearts as well.

Rembrandt paints the hands of the father, one female or mother, one male or father. It is, at once, tender and compassionate, gripping, as loving as can be imagined.

Sixteen depictions of the scene by various artists hang on the walls of my study. It is a scene that has gripped my heart and mind for many years.

If you get very still and listen, maybe you can hear the father or the mother say to the son or the daughter who has been far away, "I'm just glad you're back home." Maybe you can hear the parent say to the other son or daughter, "I love you too. Why don't you come on inside to the party? There's plenty of grace to go around." Maybe if you listen, really listen, you will catch a whisper of the voice of the One who just says to every one of us, no exceptions, "Welcome home."

No one says it better than Vincent Van Gogh, "The more I think it over, the more I feel that there is nothing more artistic than to love people."

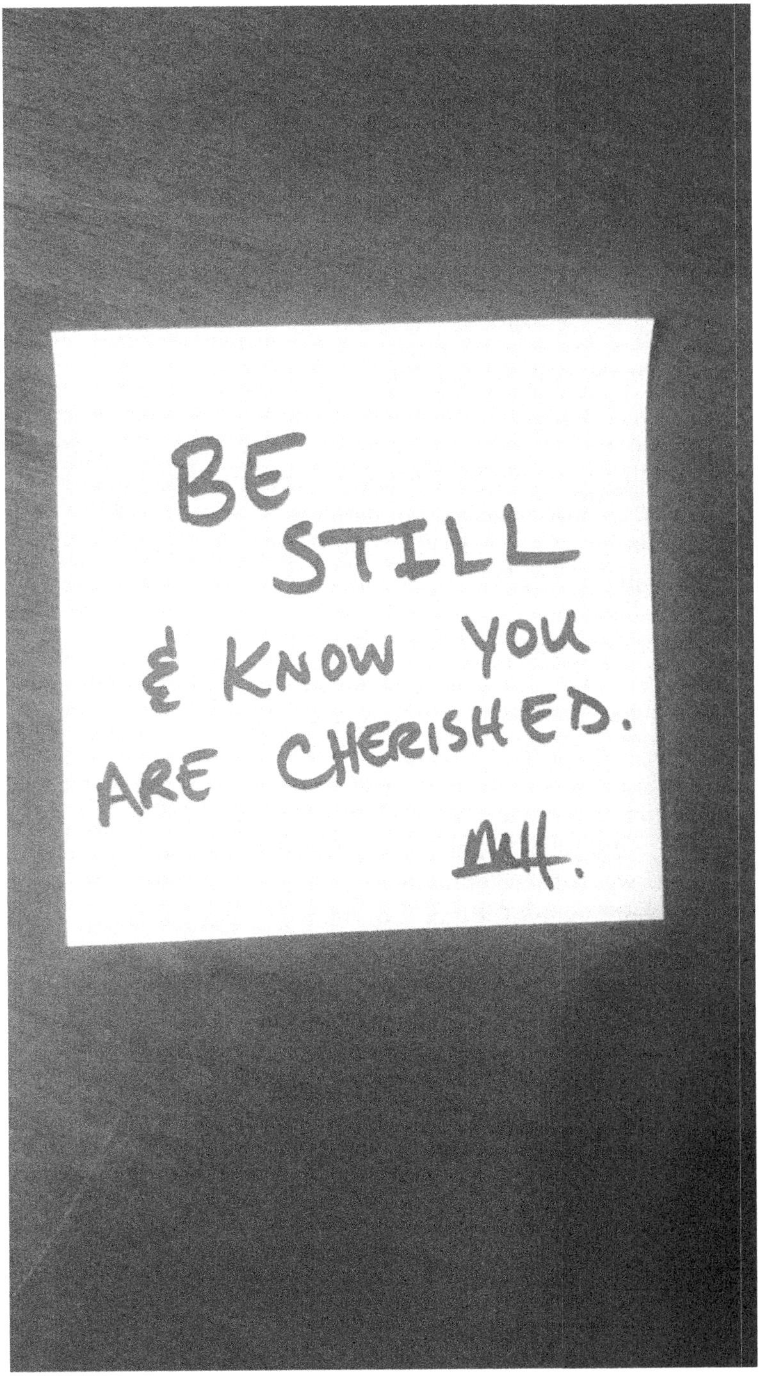
BE
STILL
& KNOW YOU
ARE CHERISHED.

March 22

To me, at my age, the main question is, "Can I be a grateful man when I die? Can I remember up to and on the last day that I had a very good life?"
—Wendell Berry

That's a mighty good question, isn't it? It reminds me of that Sunday afternoon when I was sitting with Wendell Berry on the front porch of his old farmhouse and he said, "You know, as I am aging now, my friends and I often reflect on being in a place where we have not been in the past. We don't have much point of reference for this time in our journey. It's a bit disconcerting, but I guess, every new chapter in our lives is a place we have never been."

I do not particularly like the aging process, but it is where I am now, and I want to say yes to all the seasons of my journey. I don't like my body tiring more easily now than in the past. I don't like those moments of forgetfulness. I am not fond of giving up this or that. I'd just as soon be a young man again, starting out all over. A lot of my friends say they wouldn't like to start over again. Not me. I would gladly begin all over again.

I went from childhood to manhood with not much in between. Some of it I am sure I have blocked from my memory. It is too painful to remember, and I would just as soon forget. Some of it I may have gotten entirely wrong. There were some mighty good times—great times, in fact. I just know there was also some abuse, and the wounds remain. I also know what I experienced has made me a better man.

March 23

I would just as soon put the genie back in the jar again. I know that's impossible, but still, give me back the days of my youth even if there has to be some pain. Give me back even a year or a few years. God, it has been a ride. Somebody told me the other day that I have curiosity in spades.

Maybe that's why we are given grandchildren—to see things new again. But things aren't new. Things are changing, and aging is a chapter of transition, a time of new balancing and a time to let go as well as an opportunity to dig deeper and make new discoveries. It is a time to open my hands and to be receptive to the now, this very day, I have been given.

Several of my closest friends have already departed this life, and so I want to make new friends, think new thoughts, create opportunities to drink from the wells of living water that never dry up. Victor Hugo said, "When grace is joined with wrinkles, it is adorable. There is an unspeakable dawn in old age."

"An unspeakable dawn in old age," not a sunset but a sunrise, a grace like I have never known before or will ever know exactly in this way again. Helen Keller said, "The keenness of our vision depends not on how much we can see, but on how much we feel."

March 24

When my friend Ralph Hammond, the Old Poet of Alabama, was ninety, he was still writing. He thought to title a book *The End of the Road*, but I convinced him instead to call it something else, something like another fork in the road, another new path to follow. He knew a never-ending grace, for as Jacqueline Winspear says, "Grace isn't a little prayer you chant before receiving a meal. It's a way to live."

I have been immensely blessed in my work to meet countless people who were progressing in years. I remember a man in Oklahoma who was 106 years of age. We sat at the table in his home where he lived, and he told me great stories of his life. He said, "You know, I've lived a long time, and I have two sons who are in their eighties. I don't want to outlive my sons." I think of so many other people who were living lives of profound gratitude. They were walking, eating in a healthy way, enjoying the moments. Some, of course, were struggling, and we never know what life will hand us by way of illness and infirmity, but it is as it is, and we may choose to say yes to whatever comes. Audrey Hepburn gets grace in balance with these words: "As you grow older, you will discover that you have two hands, one for helping yourself, and the other for helping others."

March 25

The other day, the muse knocked on my door, and I wrote:

The Barber's Chair

White hair
falling
in a thousand
remembrances.
Tumbling
like a runaway circus ride,
a majestic waterfall
after a summer rain.
Ah, time,
where did you go?
So swiftly fleeting.
Racing on your way.
I am a little boy.
A gentle lad
in the shadows,
waiting out the night.
I am a lonely father,
the forgotten lover,
the sometimes friend,
waiting for the morning.
Life has come to this.

March 26

These aging years of my life are times of summing up, trying to learn to relax more, to forget to carry the cell phone with me, or to be quite as accessible as I once was. I don't need to fill my life with more stuff. I need to think about what matters to me. There is an urgency now. There is a hunger for authenticity, to let my *yes* be *yes* and my *no* be *no*. I would just as soon not mince my words or say the things people want to hear. I would much rather challenge a thing or two and say in no uncertain ways what I really think.

Time is moving on more swiftly now. The train has left the station. It's not a runaway train, but there is a lot of locomotion. The duration and precise destination are unknown, but that's all right. When you are traveling on Grace Street, that's quite all right. There's music in the latter years. As the old spiritual says, "Up above my head, I hear music in the air." We may think life is about longevity, but that's not how I see it. It's about that music up above my head for whatever time I am given.

Aging exposes us, leaves nothing else to hide. Our naked bodies may not be as handsome or as beautiful as they once were, but that's all right. We can still crawl when we cannot walk, wiggle when we cannot strut, allow our imaginations to carry us anywhere we want to go. I can still sit in the dirt of my garden when I cannot bend and get myself up again.

March 27

I went to Phoenix to hear Richard Rohr, a Franciscan priest of the New Mexico province. His voice is a fresh one, calling us to authenticity and renewal. I heard him speak about his book *Falling Upward: A Spirituality for the Two Halves of Life.* It's the best book I've read on the seasons of life. You may wish to read it someday and to consider all the possibilities that lie within us, particularly in the second half of life.

My thoughts on spirituality and religion have been evolving, and what I think may evolve some more. I have fewer answers, and I am finding it is just fine to live with more of the question marks and fewer exclamation points. I used to try, in a futile attempt, to live by the letter of the law—at least, what I was convinced was the truth. Now truth comes in many packages and in many sizes and colors. Over the past few years, I have gotten it down to this—at least, for me: do justice, love mercy, walk humbly with God. I will never know precisely what Prophet Micah meant by those words, but I don't have to know. I just want to live out those words for the rest of the journey.

March 28

A friend in Idaho writes to say a very kind thing about what he observes in my life: "You have found the essence of spirituality (the perennial philosophy/wisdom) within your own tradition of Christianity; many people don't. They mistake the 'flavor' for the 'substance.'" I don't know whether his observation is true or not, but I would like to believe it and to live it.

I do know this: I am a Christian, albeit a Christian in the making, and sometimes an agnostic who thinks there is more faith in honest doubt than all the creeds of the church. I know I want to sit at a round table with people who are quite different from me. I know we all see through a glass darkly, and someday, more will be revealed. I would like a round table where we sit and listen deeply to one another. I have a vision of the Buddha sharing a mystery, the Dalai Lama smiling, Jesus and the others, welcoming all people of every race and color—lepers previously untouched, orphans so very far from home, prostitutes and beggars and liars and thieves and others who did the best they could and did, in fact, do quite well. I see no road map on the table, no book of rules or regulations, no Bible, no Koran. I see only our open hands, receptive to a grace so amazing we will never be able to comprehend though given to one and all.

We take our religion seriously but always with much humility.

March 29

I know I want to always be spending time at the potter's house where there is clay, a wheel, and the creative hands of the potter. I know I want to be molded and remolded by the refining fire of grace. I am convinced as the hymn writer put it: "O to grace how great a debtor, daily I'm constrained to be."

Annie Dillard has always been a favorite writer of mine. She speaks some remarkable words:

"There is always an enormous temptation in all of life to diddle around making itsy bitsy friends and meals and journeys for itsy bitsy years on end. It is so self-conscious, so apparently moral, simply to step aside from the gaps where the creeks and winds pour down, saying, "I never merited this grace," quite rightly, and then to sulk along the rest of your days on the edge of rage. I won't have it. The world is wider than that in all directions, more dangerous and bitter, more extravagant and bright. We are making hay when we should be making whoopee; we are raising tomatoes when we should be raising Cain, or Lazarus."

March 30

Well, a little humor now if you will indulge me as I share some prose of mine.

When I Am an Old Man

When I am an old man, I will wear flannel shirts
the year round, tightly fit around my belly.
I will put on blue polyester pants
in the summer and brown trousers
with no belt, for the rest of the year.

I will have colored socks and white ones,
some grey and pink ones, and pale blue ones
to match my trousers. When it is hot, I will wear
dark dress socks to my knees with a pair of my
favorite loud plaid shorts.
My legs will always be sexy, extraordinarily sexy.

I will turn the radio up loud
for the morning and evening news.
I will listen to the Cubs till I fall asleep.
I will forever listen for a whippoorwill
somewhere off in the night.

Every day in spring,
I will take a walk down by the creek,
sit a spell, maybe nod off against an old tree trunk,
but only if the sky is sunny and not grey.

March 31

When I am An Old Man (continued)

I wish I could go
on just one more trip in my Saturn,
somewhere brand new and exciting
Like Tennessee or Idaho.

I will eat what I darn well please.
If I had been listening to my doctors,
I would have died a long time ago.
I will have cornbread morning, noon, and night.
Raw onions and plenty of turnips and beans
will be on my kitchen table most every day.

On Friday nights, I will sip *Gentleman's Jack*
over ice in a plastic cup. I will then sleep in the buff,
especially if the temperature is below freezing.

I will sleep like a baby,
snore like a freight train,
eat prunes for breakfast,
pour a little hot sauce on my sardines,
and live what's left of my life
with as little fanfare as I can muster.

When I am an old man,
I will age well.
Exceedingly well,
I'd say.

April 1

Some years ago I began a journey of detoxification.

Religion had gotten awfully complicated - burdensome - mental gymnastics - defensive plays - all talk - God, I could pray up a storm. Plenty of answers, afraid of the questions.

The authentic ring of it just wasn't there.

I understand Philip Yancey's book, *How My Faith Survived the Church.* You do need a survival kit to traverse the obstacle course sometimes. A good dose of reality. Mostly infusions of grace and digging a little deeper. Listening doesn't hurt.

Sometimes I still play the old records like I'm not enough and I need to do something to make myself worthy and surely there are four easy steps to the promised land when really it's a lifelong process of learning to die and live.

In an illusionary world where the power belongs to the strong and it's easy to turn it all upside down, I sometimes forget that the way up is always the way down and unless a grain of wheat falls into the ground and dies, it cannot live.

I'm in the process of simplification and considering what really matters to me. You have your song to sing and I have mine and maybe in the end if we trust each other, we can learn to sing in perfect harmony -- that is, if there is perfection in our preponderance of beautiful imperfection.

April 2

Where am I? It's a good question to ask from time to time. I'm with a verse from Micah and in fact I've been there quite a number of years though I'm still learning how to shake out the wrinkles and live it out.

For me it's about doing justice in a terribly unjust world where people are beat down, showing mercy to myself and others, and being given some much needed humility in what's not a sprint but a slow and deliberate walk all way home.

It's these words on a bracelet one of my daughters gave me three years ago which have become much more than words -- rather a way to live it all out.

April 3

Through many dangers, toils and snares, I have already come,
'Tis grace hath brought me safe thus far
and grace will lead me home.
—John Newton

Mortality is not something I have come to accept easily. Only in recent years has it begun to dawn on me that I really am going to die someday. I've talked about it for years, maybe as a way of coming to terms with it. I remember that day in my doctor's office when I said something about "if I die" and she quickly corrected me, "Mr. Blake, *when* you die . . ." It's really hard to comprehend being dead. After all, I've been alive ever since I can remember.

I do not think the talk of death is a morbid thing. To dwell incessantly on it would be a different matter—unhealthy, I think. All I can do is live each and every day as fully as I can. All I can do is get up in the morning with gratitude in my heart for another day, another moment.

April 4

Nobody says it with any more clarity than Mary Oliver: "Doesn't everything die at last, and too soon. Tell me, what is your plan to do with your one wild and precious life?"

Nobody says it more beautifully than Mary Oliver: "When it is over, I want to say: all my life I was a bride married to amazement.
I was the bridegroom, taking the world into my arms."

That's it, isn't it? A bride married to amazement. A bridegroom taking the world into my arms. Maybe that's death too—this one wild and precious journey to infinity and stepping across into immortality.

Maybe that's a little part of what Plato meant when he told his students to "practice dying." Maybe every day, there is a letting go, forgetting what lies behind or ahead, and just living in the moment. Maybe we let go every day just a little more of what we have clung to so tightly.

April 5

There is a mystery in it all, isn't there? The unknown factor. I really am not looking for streets paved with gold or angels flying over my head. I just hope for a little immortality in whatever good I have breathed into my children, my grandchildren, and those others whom I have loved. I know there's DNA, but I think there is something more. There's something that remains after us when we are gone and that people never forget for as long as they live and then pass it on to those who follow us on Grace Street.

They say, no one even remembers who we were when the next generation comes along, but maybe they're wrong. Maybe something of us is written into the creation in ways I cannot articulate. Maybe you will see me again as a sunflower or a leaf falling gently to the ground or a bright and sunny morning after the night has passed and you feel that certain peace in your heart.

I read an article once in the Goshen, Indiana, newspaper that tore me to pieces. Maybe the writer says what a lot of us feel:

"I am surrounded by life and death. It is stacked above me into the sky. It is anchored below me in earth and in water. When I think about the truth that I will have to do what all living things do, I am sometimes left bleak and breathless. Other times I feel desperate to do something—anything—to remind the future people that I was once alive. I have to stop and see myself for what I am: A decent, unremarkable kind of person, who is going to live and die like all the other decent, unremarkable people. I feel some shame admitting that this fate doesn't seem good enough for me. I guess I'm not alone in wanting a larger effect."

April 6

"A larger effect"—maybe Martin Luther King's words are true after all: "Life's most persistent and urgent question is: What are you doing for others?" I think we can pretty well take care of ourselves; it's how we are taking care of others that also matters.

Give me over and over again what James Baldwin has to say about death:

"Perhaps the whole root of our trouble, the human trouble, is that we will sacrifice all the beauty of our lives, will imprison ourselves in totems, taboos, crosses, blood sacrifices, steeples, mosques, races, armies, flags, nations, in order to deny the fact of death, the only fact we have. It seems to me that one ought to rejoice in the fact of death—ought to decide, indeed, to earn one's death by confronting with passion the conundrum of life."

Amen and preach it, James Baldwin. It's about confronting with passion the conundrum of life and facing death, the only fact we have.

April 7

I think death brings us into a clearing. Always there is a clearing. No matter how great the night, the darkness is dispelled and the light forever outlasts the darkness. As the writer says, "Yet even at the grave we make our song: Alleluia, Alleluia, Alleluia."

I remember the words of T. S. Eliot in "East Coker" --

> Old men ought to be explorers
> Here and there does not matter
> We must be still and still moving
> Into another intensity
> For another union, a deeper communion.

I like the way the monks at the Abbey of Gethsemani see death with just the name and date of death on small white crosses. They say, that date is the all-consuming date.

When I die, say I have pitched my tent in a land called hope, not hopelessness, doubt, despair, loneliness, hostility, or cynicism. Say I was a prodigal son who saw my father running down the road after me when I was far from home. Say my father, our father, loved me with an unimagined love and would not let me go. Say it's morning. Say I'm home.

April 8

As Lewis Smedes writes, "Grace is the gift of feeling sure that our future, even our dying, is going to turn out more splendidly than we dare imagine."

It has been a great ride! And with traveling mercies, I hope my story of grace will go on into the future. I would like there to be other chapters. I desire more forks in the road, and with Robert Frost, I ask to take the road less traveled. With Dylan Thomas, I want to "rage, rage against the dying of the light."

I've been thinking about the words for the little gravestone where my ashes will be buried. For many years, I have tried to think of something like "God is faithful."

But the years as they have come and gone have changed my way of seeing it. Just have chiseled in the stone, "Traveling on Grace Street."

April 9

I say grace over almost everything.
—Jack Gilbert

When the doctor said *cancer*, it never occurred to me to surrender.

Quite the contrary, it was my reveille, my moment to get up and walk or crawl if need be. I want to travel on Grace Street for as long as I am given.

This street is one that I am familiar with because it has become the geography of my heart. It is the unfolding of a long journey, a widening path, and a clearing in which I intend to travel for as long as I have breath.

Someone says my voice is strong and has taken on a new knowing. That may be true, but I am often weak. There are moments when I feel like fainting and I am weary. I am a man of clay feet. Life has its twists and turns, and the sooner we get into the flow of it, the better. Life is about consistently being in a growth mode.

April 10

Life is about saying yes to whatever is flung in our direction and making the necessary adjustments to stay on the road for the entirety of the journey, always a journey full of surprises and unexpected gifts. Stipulated, there have been some detours along the way. I have my regrets but not too many. I wish I had been a more grace-filled man. There have been some bridges to cross on a path to authenticity. I wish my walk had matched my talk in more definitive ways, but those dusty roads are left behind and I am heading home.

My medical condition, the doctor says, is chronic, serious, and treatable. None of us know the longevity of our lives, but all of us can live with the hope that is within us. We are surrounded by those who love us and who walk with us every step of the way. We live somewhere between the old twins of fear and hope, with the scales tipping decidedly in the direction of hope. This moment is a nudge forward, a reaching for my own words as to what to say and to write. It is at once liberating, therapeutic, and healing to put words to paper.

April 11

Grace is all around us and in us. Grace permeates all people everywhere who inhabit the earth. Our purpose, our one great purpose, is to learn to love each other and this magnificent world, all creatures great and small, with which we are one.

The author of these words is debatable, but the idea is clear: "When writing the story of your life, don't let anyone else hold the pen."

We understand. We must speak in our own unique voice and be as honest as we know how to be, remembering that we all see through a glass darkly. Later on, we may see clearly.

And while I hold the pen, there are other scribes of grace who join in the writing, the chorus. I hear their voices. I see their faces. Their stories move me. I am in their debt, and as always, I am in your debt, fellow traveler, for walking alongside me on Grace Street.

April 12

It's cancer.
-My oncology surgeon

I sit in a room and hear an oncology surgeon say, "You have a melanoma in the deeper part of your back." And then he adds, "You know that's cancer." I blink and think; of course I know that's cancer, the third confirmed melanoma in six months but let me back up.

It started simply enough a few weeks before Christmas. The dermatologist observed, "There's a place just below your temple on the right side of your face with some variation of color. It has to be removed and biopsied." The doctor takes it out, stitches me up, and says, "You'll hear from me in a week."

A few hours later a grandson quips, "You'll be Scarface."

I am surprised when the doctor calls. Yes, a melanoma, but very surface. "We got it early. You should be fine, but we'll have to check you every three months for two years and then every six months for the rest of your life." I feel lucky, fortunate, blessed. All the grandchildren are coming for Christmas.

I put my entire physical house in order just after the holidays.

My spiritual house has been in order for a very long time, but I can't get enough of the woods, the birds, and the creation, and I talk to every monk at a couple of monasteries who is willing to talk. The monks talk about what matters. Maybe it is because they live close to the earth.

April 13

There's Ash Wednesday in the liturgical calendar of the Christian year. Always a moving day in my journey. "Ashes to ashes, dust to dust," and someone says, "It's the only time we ever attend our own funeral."

Silly man, why you talk of dyin' so much? Maybe it's my way of trying to come to terms with my mortality whenever it comes and not deny it or try to run away from it.

I see a place on my arm and panic. "Mr. Blake, this is nothing, but if it will make you feel better, I'll take it off." Yes, take it off. I feel ridiculous for wanting it off my skin.

A week passes and I feel a tiny bump on my back but think it's nothing. I'm fine. I'll wait till my next appointment in the spring to have it checked. I've already embarrassed myself once over nothing.

In the spring, the dermatologist question, "How long have you had this?"

"Three months," I say. He says, "It's nothing but we have to take it out and have it biopsied."

Since I am driving to Kentucky to see my family and the dressing has to be changed twice a day, I ask, "Can we wait a week or so?"

"Yes," the doctor says. We both think it's nothing.

Kentucky is wonderful. I spend the day at the Abbey of Gethsemani with my friend Bill Laramee. We walk in the woods; we talk of family and friends and what matters. I see all my closest friends who have been lights in my journey for many years.

April 14

I bird-watch with my grandson. I see everyone in my family except a son-in-law who is in Canada on business and my daughter-in-law who has to stay home with a grandson who is sick.

She bakes me a birthday cake and everybody sings but the little ones don't know how to place the numbers on the cake. *Is it 76 or 67?* they muse.

Back in Georgia, the place on my back is removed. It's nothing. Two weeks pass and the dermatologist finally calls and it's something. "This is a concern," he says. "The pathologist thinks there is also a melanoma deeper in your back. You will have to have your eyes examined by an ophthalmologist. People get melanomas in their eyes. We've set you up for a MRI of your brain and a CT scan at Emory University Hospital tomorrow, but come to my office today. I want to check your body thoroughly."

I lie butt-naked on a narrow pad while he examines every twist and turn of my body. "Turn over slowly and be careful. We don't want you to fall off the board." That's funny and he has said that on other occasions.

When you are naked, you surrender. There is no place to hide. The doctor walks me to my car and I think this is unusual and he tells me, "We will be with you all through this time." Later he calls, this consummate professional, and says, "Mr. Blake, I love you and I am praying for you," and I am moved to tears.

I wait in crowded waiting rooms. A good name for those rooms, I think. I see people. I see faces. They are all just like me, fellow travelers on a journey, some with much greater needs than mine. All of us, one family, struggling to make it home. One family.

April 15

"You want a headset to listen to some music during the MRI of your brain?" the technician questions.

"Sure."

"What kind of music you want?" she asks. "Give me classical or Southern gospel," I answer. The headset doesn't work and my nose is a couple of inches away from a cylinder as she photographs my brain. Should I smile or say "cheese"? I wonder.

I remember the surgery to remove a blood clot on my brain three years ago. I meditate quietly in the machine on the Scripture: "Be still and know that I am God."

The MRI is over and I wait for about two hours to have the full body scan. The technician injects the dye in my arm and I drink some chocolate-mix "stuff," and he tells me, "Just like mocha at Starbucks," and he also says I am radioactive, and if I go to the airport, I should be sure to let security know.

We laugh. He stands to leave the room, and I think, This doesn't taste like Starbucks, while he says he will be back in an hour when I am fully "active" and take me across the hall for the scan. Finally it is done. Smile or say "cheese"? still I wonder.

Two days later, four injections go into the melanoma in the deeper part of my back to track where the drainage goes and where lymph nodes will be removed. The radiologist is great joy. We talk about what matters. She tells me about her two-year-old son, the love of her life. She tells me there are "hot spots" the doctor will see. Maybe the cancer has spread or maybe not.

A guy named John, who will help put me to sleep, asks, "You ready to get this done?"

"Yes, I am!"

April 16

I am rolled into surgery. John put one thumb up, and I put two thumbs up and think of my grandson's prayer for me—"Dear God, please be with granddaddy today and keep him safe and give him peace. Amen"—and I am out for the count till I wake up in recovery after the removal of a massive tumor in my back along with the excising of three lymph nodes.

"I'll tell you in ten days about the biopsy of those three lymph nodes. Fifty percent chance of survival if they are cancerous. Seventy-five percent chance of survival if they are not," the doctor says in a matter-of-fact way, but I privately pondered what percentages mean anyway and why is everything in ten days.

My friends tell me those removed lymph nodes are not cancer. I say that I honestly do not know. Only God knows.

Three incisions, one in my back and two under my arms, are uncomfortable. How do I lie in bed? What do I do with this chapter in the journey? How do I say yes to whatever life hands me? A friend gives me a homemade card. "The birds just don't seem to sound as sweet when you are not feeling well. Get well soon, Jeff!"

April 17

Cathy Edgett, outside San Francisco, assisted in writing *Traveling on Grace Street* and wrote a book about the unexpected gifts of cancer in her own life, and I wonder how this could ever possibly be, these gifts.

Don't be afraid. It will be all right. Hold out your hands and accept the gifts. Whatever happens, there are these gifts.

Helen Harvey, outside Washington, DC, shares with me some words from her daughter: "Life is going to throw you challenges. You will feel what you feel. But remember to take a second look. In every challenge you face, there is a gift. Look for it. Because it may be the most treasured gift you ever find."

I hope for better news. I have chronic, serious or aggressive (depending on which oncologist is speaking), and treatable cancer. Which words should I hold or latch on to in the mix of all?

I begin the wait for more surgery, this time the removal of more than thirty additional lymph nodes and to determine if the cancer has spread. That will come in a few days and will be another piece of the puzzle.

April 18

Where's my inspiration? So very many people and places, so much poetry, so many words from the books I treasure, as well as lovely walks in nature, the sunflowers, the human and the spiritual, which are one and the same. There are those nine grandchildren, my lights.

I do not know anyone who wants to overly indulge in thoughts about the fragility of life, but it can be a healthy and positive exercise, a way of remembering as the old spiritual says, "Up above my head, I hear music in the air," and in a mystical sort of way, there is a current, more than a thread of grace, which we never quite comprehend, that carries us along the way.

It is a matter of jumping into the water. We are flesh-and-blood mortality/immortality, which means we embrace each and every moment we are given as a priceless gift.

Robert Burns, the Scottish poet, reminds us that "the best laid schemes of mice and men often go awry." Most of us have long since realized in our false/true selves that we are broken vessels with kinks in our armor. Our vessels leak and our armor has "cracks where the light gets in," as Leonard Cohen sings.

We have "not yet" places that remind us that we need each other as well as all the other resources at our fingertips in this tiny vessel, this earth ship, on which we are sailing through deep waters.

Life shockingly turns on something as small as the head of a pin.

April 19

Our expectations are turned upside down by some circumstance we never imagined.

The invincibility we thought we had leaves the station like a runaway train, and we are shaken to our senses, aware of the fact that we are in need of something more than our own ingenuity to make it through the hard places and finally get to higher ground.

Grace comes to us in unexpected places we never imagine.

April 20

"Vanity of vanities, all is vanity," the writer says, which is to say, there is more to life than the vanity of the temporal or that which we can only see or touch.

Vulnerability/fragility means staying awake for as long as our bodies and minds will permit us to do so. It means getting into the flow of the spiritual dimensions by which we may choose to live. Call those dimensions what you will. There is something more to the journey than the celebration of the self.

The natural order, nature itself, can be a great teacher along the various paths we travel and can point us in the direction of something more.

Henry David Thoreau writes in his statement of purpose in the second chapter of *Walden*—"We must learn to reawaken and keep ourselves awake, not by mechanical aids, but by an infinite expectation of the dawn, which does not forsake us in our soundest sleep."

Half-asleep as I write these words, I look out my window to the world and see a red-bellied woodpecker at one of my feeders. He startles me awake, fully awake to the possibilities of each and every day to accept and be grateful for my vulnerability, my fragility, and to embrace every moment of what I hope will be a long journey home.

Thoreau also says, "Every man is the builder of a temple, called his body, to the god he worships, after a style purely his own, nor can he get off by hammering marble instead. We are all sculptors and painters, and our material is our own flesh and blood and bones."

April 21

I am reminded of John Bunyan's *Pilgrim's Progress*. I cannot recall the names of the two characters in Bunyan's writing, but I do know they are traveling through rough waters.

One says to the other, "I can feel the bottom and it is steady."

When we walk through deep waters, and most of us will at one time or another, it is good to know the ground is steady and that we are always kept in the hands of the God, who is all love, all faithfulness, all grace.

Richard Rohr speaks, "Your life is not about you. You are about life."

May I say, our lives are not about us.

Our lives are about grace.

April 22

    In the midst of the darkness and light, there is a near-perfect evening as I sit under a canopy of stars and listen to a symphony of crickets and tree frogs.

    The gentle cool breeze, the buttery full moon, and the quietness and solitude are all there, and the only response necessary is to open my hands and receive. There's a new book I'm reading, *Paradise in Plain Sight*. It's true, isn't it?

    A friend quotes scripture to me, and I think all my life I have been inspired by many sacred and secular writings. Vast wells of wisdom, insight, and discovery are always at our fingertips. The words are those of the apostle who writes, "Not only so, but we also rejoice in our sufferings, because we know that suffering produces perseverance; perseverance, character; and character, hope. And hope does not disappoint us, because God has poured out his love into our hearts by the Holy Spirit, whom he has given us."

April 23

What a magnificent journey from suffering to perseverance to character to hope.

Some of healing is a mystery and we see through a glass darkly.

Most everything I know contemporaneously about healing comes from the life and writings of Frank Stanger and E. Stanley Jones.

Stanger was a professor of mine who had a complete physical and mental collapse at the top of his profession and came out of the valley, stronger than ever.

Jones suffered a paralyzing stroke when he was in his late eighties. It was then that he wrote one of his greatest books, *The Divine Yes.*

I learn from Stanger the meaning of three simple words: "God wills wholeness." He repeats those words over and over again until I begin to see that God is never the author of sickness or suffering and that God's great desire is for us to be whole, but the truth is, some people get well and some people do not; thus there is mystery and the unknown. And the even greater truth is known, and it is ultimately, even as we walk the long valley earth side, there will come a day of wholeness. Sometimes the timetable is not our timetable.

I learn from Jones how to walk through the night and to say yes to God regardless. We may tremble and shake on the rock, the old spiritual says, but the rock never shakes under us. I do not have to plead with God or beg God or be exceedingly anxious ultimately because I am being made whole at every juncture of the journey, and I can say yes regardless.

April 24

With Camus, I discover, "In the midst of winter, I found there was, within me, an invincible summer."

My son reminds me of a young friend of his whose beautiful daughter was terribly ill and ultimately died. He gave my son this bit of guidance: "Be careful what you pray for, Blake. Just surrender everything into God's hands."

If you want to talk about faith, that's how I see faith.

My sister speaks about eagles. She says that eagles climb above the storm and soar. I later read that an eagle can climb up to ten thousand feet and survive. Isn't that a great story?

Sometimes we soar above the storm, and sometimes we walk right on ahead through the storm. I know it is easier, smoother sailing above it all, but I also know some of the deepest experiences of my life have come by walking through the storm.

Don't you think that, if there was a magic formula for all healing, there would be a patent on it already? Don't you think, if "mustard seed" faith worked every time, we would all be growing mustard in our gardens and bottling up all our faith in a jar?

And isn't it great to have people with us who soar like eagles or grab hold of our hands and just keep on walking with us through hell or high water?

April 25

I don't know any of us who are not in need of some kind of healing.

Since we are body, mind, and spirit, most of us realize a need for physical, emotional, or spiritual healing at one time or another. We want to be made whole, but we have our broken places, our wounds, and our need for mending when life hands us first one and then another challenge.

In the middle of the night, I see in my mind and heart the people in my own circle who need healing and I have images of them being made whole as I and others pray for them. I remember a woman in her eighties who underwent nine hours of surgery; a young lad with a failing transplanted kidney, which causes me to question God as to why such a sweet boy suffers; a sister with blockages in her arteries who will have her heart explored again; and a woman I simply saw in passing while I was on my way to pre-op as she sat alone, ashen and pale, in a room while some chemical was entering her arm, and our eyes met and she reached out to me in her pain; a friend a little younger than me who is essentially immobilized but whose spirit soars; my grandson, so very young, who has known more than his share of trouble but who takes charge of any room he enters, unconscious of his disability; and a fellow who is addicted to heroin and alcohol. I know people who are addicted to prescription drugs and beloved men whose minds are slipping away.

We're a family with wounds. We need healing when we are estranged from family members or suffer damaged emotions and can't seem to let go of the past or when we stand beside people we love who are suffering as we help lift them up. In countless ways, we need healing. We are called to be wounded healers.

April 26

We are sometimes sick in our politics shooting our wounded.
We do not wait for military justice to sort out and we judge a soldier coming home from Afghanistan. We rip out his stitches, suspect his family, and use him as a pawn in our perverted politics. We are the sick ones who would rather destroy our country than come to common ground.

We are sometimes sick in our religion. We accept sugarcoated pills that will ultimately kill our spirits. We drink the purple Kool-Aid, which stunts our growth and keeps us from being who we are intended to be. We want magic and call it a prayer for the miraculous. We believe the lies we are told about our worthlessness, our evilness. All lies. We believe in the power of positive thinking, but sometimes thinking fails when we would do well to center on a word from an apostle:

"Whatever is true, whatever is noble, whatever is right, whatever is pure, whatever is lovely, whatever is admirable—if anything is excellent or praiseworthy—think about such things."

April 27

Here's what I believe -- We are all held in the hands of a spirit, a being, another, a god, or by whatever name we choose to use and that on our way home we are being made whole in a love that never lets us go or leaves us alone.

I think of Scott Peck's profound first sentence in his book *The Road Less Traveled*: "Life is difficult." Peck says, once we truly see this truth, we transcend it, and I remember the first of the four noble truths, which Buddha taught: "Life is suffering."

Grace is the unmistakable knowledge that we are being healed.

April 28

When I had my first consultation with a new oncology physician, I liked her instantly.

"We all put our little blinders on and pretend," she says, and then she adds, "I am glad, Mr. Blake, you have such a love for life that you are going through this with clarity and that every day for you is a gift."

The journey has a way, if we will allow it to do so, of removing our pretense and stripping us of our blinders.

The birds have never sung more sweetly; the garden has never flourished so well. The poetry and prose overflow, the relationships that matter, all matter. The walks in the woods sustain me. Meditation, centering, and prayer are like rivers of life.

I am not much different than the next guy. The last time I looked, my feet are made of clay. I stumble and struggle. I laugh and I cry. And there are people, people everywhere, who suffer much more than my little sufferings have been. It is to those others who suffer that my heart goes out in solidarity every day.

We walk by faith and not by sight on this magnificent journey home.

April 29

We do not have all the answers, nor do we need to know all there is to know for we are in the hands of the Greater One. It is sufficient, more than sufficient to know, that grace sustains us every step of the way.

My ancestry has little or nothing to do with the man I am today. I have an uncle, a Blake, who took a gun out in the front yard of his rural home and sat in a chair under a tree and blew his brains out because he could not endure the pain or face the music of cancer anymore.

What sustains me? I have had long years of seeking and finding, learning, growing, failing, stumbling, discovering, excelling, and exposing myself to a great big world of diversity, with the realization that we are all one family on earth, all creatures great and small, and that we have come from dust and will return to dust.

What a wonderful journey through the valleys, up the mountains, and around the bends, to discover yet something else that is new and exciting and profoundly enriching.

What sustains me? My family and my friends—actually all the people of the earth, our fellow-travelers, who are the human face of God.

April 30

What Remains

After chance and change and circumstance,
have their way with us and we take
our walk across the stage of life
like actors in a Shakespeare play,
I wonder what remains.

After struggle and fear and doubt,
seasons of our journeys in the now,
and we stumble, crawl, run the race
with unexpected, joy-filled abandonment,
I wonder what remains.

After the battle scars, the question marks,
the not-yet places which are common to all of us,
our brush with sensuality, spirituality,
Eros or God or both and what is between,
I wonder what remains.

After the sprint to the finish line,
embracing life as the splendid gift,
passing through on borrowed ground,
on the edge of unimagined grace,
what remains?

Solid ground. Sifting sand. .
Rich in things. Poor in spirit.
Empty hands. Love-spent lives.
Fear and hope.
What remains?

May 1

To the memory of Albert Jefferson Blake, Jr
Beloved Father

A Purple Heart

He fights a thousand demons of hell on the bloody fields
of Germany. Barely a man, so far from home, he prays to
the God of the night and cries like a boy for the break of day.

There are no whippoorwills. No cotton fields. There are no
watermelons on the vine. No home-made biscuits from his
mother's hand. No sweet kisses or hugs from his lovely bride.

Only a lonely foxhole. There is the stench of rotting bodies
in the town. There is a dagger with a swastika taken from a dead
Nazi solider. Nothing more than rations from a can.

Peace, peace, there is no peace. There shall be war and
rumors of war. They hammer their plowshares into swords.
Their greed, their lust for flesh and blood, betray their hollow,
empty words.

Only a Purple Heart from a grateful nation on the day he
turns nineteen. Only a dusty memory in a shadowbox of a man
bruised, battered, broken, fighting the demons of hell.

May 2

To the memory of Doris Traylor Blake - Beloved Mother

She Waited Till Spring

She could have left us in winter when the earth was quiet in lower light.

Or in autumn when the woods were laughing at death, showing out, and covering earth in a tapestry of gold, yellow, and crimson red.

Or in summer when the fiery Southern sun was searing down on the land and the air was heavy, laden in grief.

But, no, she waited till spring when the jonquils had long since heralded the changing season, the robins were out, and the cardinals had flown across the river.

She waited till the azaleas were in bloom, the dogwood foretold resurrection, the wisteria draped the trees in the color purple, the redbuds were all over the woods, and the grass was lush and green.

She waited till she waged her last battle and her struggle was over. I know the moment she surrendered, resting her head on my hand, our hearts in unbroken love.

She had already danced her last waltz, made her last journey to some distant land, and sung for joy from somewhere deep within but way off-key, "Jesus loves me – this I know."

She waited till spring when the whole creation sings, when children sing, "Alleluia."   -129-

May 3

Little Girls on a Sunday Morn
16th Street Baptist Church, Birmingham, Alabama 9-15-1963

Little girls on a Sunday morn.
Giggling and wiggling and trying on robes.
Not a care in the world, not a cloud in the sky.
Safe and secure from all alarm.

Little girls on a Sunday morning.
Giggling and wiggling and trying to pray.
God's in his heaven, not a worry or fret.
Childlike, unbound, such a carefree day.

Little girls on a Sunday morn.
Giggling and wiggling and about to die.
Their innocent blood splattered on walls.
Bomb blasted into eternity's arms.

Little girls on a Sunday morn.
Murdered by Klansmen with dynamite.
Evil cowards, demented, these beasts,
Unimagined terror in God's house that day.

Little girls on a Sunday morn.
Lie mortally wounded in rubble and smoke.
Stained glass window with Christ's face blown out.
Crucify him, crucify him.
My God, my God, why?

Little girls on a Sunday morn.
While sobbing mothers can only cry,
My baby, my baby,
My baby, why?

May 4

Kentucky Sunrise

I have always loved this time of day
and this Kentucky home of mine.
The entire horizon, almost in sight
as black turns gray then faint and light.
Sitting here, pressed against the window, I see
the rolling hills, the curing barn, the robin nesting,
the wobbly-legged foal nursing at a mother's
breast who will not run for the roses today.
I see the shadow of a gentle breeze
blowing across the pastures so fertile, so green.
Somewhere last night, a boy dreamed of hoops
and cheers while crowds roared "Kentucky Blue."
Somewhere just now, a miner in the hills went down
beneath the earth to dig for coal in tunnels dark.
I see the seasons come and go, the deep fallen snow
now quiet, so quiet, the frolicking horses on the farm
in spring when time stands still, so still.
I see the fence of stone, the old meandering river and wile
away the day. I watch the workers plant tobacco one by one
in the fallow fields. I hear the music of simple gifts
and feel free – yes free – this fine Kentucky morn.

May 5

Kentucky Spring

There is nothing like a Kentucky spring.
Every living thing awakens from the dead,
rising in splendid silence before my senses.

I want to bow down low and touch the earth.
It is as though my heart skips a beat. A sigh
of joy comes over me. I catch my breath.

The dark slumbering season of winter ends
and nature is aroused, stirring like Lazarus,
on another endless resurrection morning.

May 6

Latter Years

There is urgency now. The steps are quickened,
firm, with only occasional drift, in this autumn season.

Time is moving swiftly like a train. Not run-a-way, rather,
with steady speed, traveling to an anticipated destination.

There is a deeper hunger for authenticity, for solid rock in
sifting, shallow, fleeting sand while absorbing what remains.

Sight may fail, but scales covering blinded eyes are fewer now.
The treasure is found in a leaky earthen vessel, yet treasure still.

Waiting is easier than before. Why not give the ripened grapes
the time they need to ferment and borrow not from needless
fear?

This is the quiet, listening time of intensification which stretches
to the grave. The awe and wonder will not diminish with
passing light.

The embrace is longer. Moments are really all that matter. There
is no time left to harbor ill or to carry grudges, guilt or shame.

There is a presence, a cloud of knowing, a reality, a refining fire
which flickers but is rekindled in the night, celebrating changing
seasons.

There is music in the latter years.

May 7

My Alabama Home

I see a thousand falling stars at night
falling, falling from sky
on this my Alabama Home.
I see a steel mill belching smoke.
I hear a whippoorwill.
There goes a dove, a quail, a deer.
I see the Iron Man on the hill.
I smell a paper mill.
I see the cotton pickers and their bags.
The neighbors raise a barn.
I walk along the pristine bay.
I look for arrowheads in the fields
where Creek and Cherokees once roamed.
Helen Keller says, "Water" simply "Water"
and her dark night is turned to day.
I hear a deep South, Southern drawl.
A canopy of kudzu blankets every hill.
There's gospel music on the radio:
"Rock of Ages, cleft for me. Let me
hide myself in Thee."
My neighbor has a banjo on his knee.
The world's space frontier begins right here.
I see the antebellum homes, the magnolias
in their bloom, the dogwoods and azaleas
everywhere in spring.
The watermelons are to eat, "but not before the Fourth."
There's okra, squash, corn, tomatoes, and
so much more. There's pecan pie, sweet potato pie,
banana puddin', a table spread.

May 8

My Alabama Home (continued)

I hear the sound of a bomb, or screams, of dogs,
of fear. They ride the bus, they cross the bridge,
and shed their blood, martyrs for a noble cause.
I hear his thunderous voice from Dexter Avenue.

I love these rivers; the Alabama, the Coosa,
the Tombigbee, the Tennessee. I love the fall
when leaves turn gold and yellow and crimson red.

I miss the Bear and the gridiron duel.
I miss Bethel on a hill, the old cemetery out back.
I miss Thanksgiving at Mama's house.
I miss playing dominoes and rook.
I miss Grandmother on Christmas Day.

I hear Hank Williams and his mournful song
about a poor old Indian brave who never got a kiss.
So many places on this earth I have roamed. So much
I have seen and learned. So many people have crossed
my path and taught me on the way. But in the quiet
stillness of this hour, I still remember home.

My Alabama home.

May 9

A Sycamore Tree at Gethsemani

In the place that I am home
there stands a sycamore tree.
More years than I remember
I have rested in its arms,
thought to bow in its presence.

The tree's maker is God.
A mystic sweet communion
grows between heaven and earth.
Its sacred ground not far
from where the brothers sleep.

Sleeping the blessed sleep.
White crosses along the rolling hills.
Only a single holy date
marking immortality's full circle
where all the people of all the ages live.

A solitary tree lives in silence.
Only the monastery bells
and the sun and the rain
break the solitude
where nature's prayers are lifted.

The branches of the tree are massive.
Like expansive wings of ancient birds.
The great lover's encompassing embrace.
All inclusive, never refusing or denying.
All love, all loves excelling.

May 10

A Sycamore Tree at Gethsemani (continued)

The Kentucky wind blows in winter
and the darkest night falls
and the morning always breaks
and the robin builds her nest
as seasons come and go.

God makes the limbs of the tree
a place for birds to sing,
to rest from flight,
to gaze on earth.
To join the chorus of Grace.

The tree's layered bark falls away
like egos must fall away.
The work is to rest.
To breathe, to breathe.
To surrender to the Now.

I hear the Teacher say,
'Zaccheus, you come down.'
Come down.
Deep roots grow here.
Bow down.

May 11

Ode to Grace
    The Abbey of Gethsemani, Trappist, Kentucky

I ran slowly from your suffocating arms
the first night we met many years ago.
I was afraid of your silence,
your otherness,
For you see, I am both sons,
Prodigal and elder,
Free spirit of the wind
and lost in the dead law.
Living in the shadows,
yet so very hungry for your light.

Since the first night we met,
I have been running back to you,
running and leaping and dancing,
like the prodigal coming home,
or a wayward child reaching
and finding his mother or father,
a ship tossing at sea
hoping to make harbor,
a broken reed
in need of healing,
a sunflower
thirsty for the sun.

May 12

Ode to Grace (Continued)

When the heavens were as brass,
You found me.
Through all darkness,
You saw me.
Pulling up a thousand roots,
You anchored me.
In this cracked earthen vessel,
in my altogether holy earthiness,
You discovered me.
This is my home.
Your heart is my geography.
Remember me.
I know your name.
Your name is Grace.

May 13

The Dream

Written on the 40th Anniversary of the Selma March on the road
between Selma and Montgomery, Alabama

Not by a pillar of fire or an unknown cloud
in the far-flung sky,
nor by some other sign
from God above, but by the still small voice,
consuming flame within,
I embrace this sacred journey,
this mission of remembrance,
and recommit myself to the dream.

May 14

Marco Pullis says, "This is in fact the function of grace . . . to condition men's homecoming to the center." Ah, to live each and every day in the center and the center is grace. The center is love.

I affirm the words of Barbara Brown Taylor when she says, "What is saving my life now is becoming more fully human, trusting that there is no way to God apart from real life in the real world."

There are moments when I have wavered and questioned. I had my doubts as to how this story would progress and what the results would be. I understand what Paul Tillich, the theologian and philosopher, meant when he wrote, "Doubt is not the opposite of faith; it is one element of faith."

I do not believe there is one cure for all. Illness and suffering are the lot of the entire human family, just as healing and wholeness are part of what it means to be human, and somewhere in the middle of it all, there is mystery, the unknown.

We are being made and remade over and over again.

It's like a beautiful tapestry. The part we see is often quite lovely. It may be a work of art that takes our breath away. There is the beauty of imagination and wonder expressed on the exposed side of the tapestry, but if you observe the other side, there may be an entanglement of threads running in all directions. And so it is with life, so it is with our journeys.

May 15

Sometimes it takes a while, maybe a lifetime, to understand all the twists and turns, the mountains and valleys, through which we travel on our way home. Why am I being allowed to go on living a while longer? I do not know the answer to that question, but I believe I will look back and understand it better by and by.

All I know for sure is that my life is profoundly changed because of what I have experienced in illness and suffering, and I count it all joy to know that grace has sustained me every step of the way.

What a gift, what an incredible gift. None of us are promised tomorrow, but we are promised more grace than we could ever imagine for every step of the way. We, as Thich Nhat Hanh puts it, "have an appointment with life."

I go back to the woods, to the birds of the air, to my garden, to my grandchildren, to great music and art, to books that stir my mind and heart, to photography, to writing, and most of all, to those people who are just like me in the common need we share to be loved in this one world, this one family, this one great pulsating life that is molding us and making us and renewing us.

Oh my! What a journey.

May 16

Where thou art, that is home.
—Emily Dickinson

More than forty years ago my beloved grandmother died. I cannot remember being in the old house in the country near Equality, Alabama, very much after her death or when my grandfather moved away.

My grandparents lived in the red clay country of central Alabama on a farm, which was my favorite place on earth when I was a boy. My memories are mostly delightful, immensely wonderful in fact, except for a few times when there was trouble in the family. I could go on a while about the good times. We fished and swam in the cool water pond and heard the sweet melodies of the birds. We played dominos. My grandfather and I ate watermelon right out in his patch on hot summer days and I learned to spit seeds. He took me everywhere in his green 1940 Ford pickup truck. I sat in the seat beside him as we bumped along. What times we had—eating homemade biscuits piping hot from the oven every morning in a kitchen filled with the aroma of a baked-to perfection delight, getting a nickel to buy bubblegum when the Rolling Store came along the country road, drinking a dipper of cool water from the well or drinking a glass of homemade blackberry wine in later years with my grandmother, just a few weeks before she died.

Her voice was sweet and kind and gentle, and I hear it often. I see her loving eyes. Mama Blake was my favorite person in the whole wide world.

Grace is very often precious memories.

May 17

Some time ago, I went back to the house where my grandparents lived, no longer a home, only a shell of a dwelling, and it all was immensely sad. When the home was sold, I do not believe anyone ever lived in it again.

The front door was open, and I walked in to observe a gutted house. Ceilings and walls destroyed. Debris everywhere. Birds roosting everywhere. The stench was sickening.

I tried to imagine the way it used to be. I imagined the old clock on the mantle, the creak of the rocking chairs, the churn where my grandmother made butter, the oven where she baked the best biscuits I ever ate, and the radio where we listened to Southern gospel music. I thought of big Thanksgiving and Christmas family gatherings, but the laughter, wonder, and joy-filled moments that I saw with my little boy eyes were all gone.

There was no family gathering. No aunts and uncles and cousins around the table. There was no prayer from my grandfather's lips: "Gracious Lord, Give us humble and true hearts for these together and all other blessings. I ask for Christ's sake. Amen."

It was all gone. Gone with time and age and decay as a generation slips away to ultimately be remembered no more in graves where there are no flowers. There is only the peace of knowing they are in the arms of God.

Roots and branches are important. I have been connected in a mystical, marvelous way with my past. I am forever enriched and changed by my current home places on Grace Street.

May 18

I used to question and doubt Thomas Wolfe's title *You Can't Go Home Again.*

Sure you can, I have thought, but I am not so sure anymore. Time like an ever-flowing stream moves on, and the whole world changes. I guess I preferred a memory, half fantasy and half reality. And where is home? I've been searching for home for a very long time.

I've been traveling on Grace Street on the way home.

I have been a kind of a seeker, a discoverer on a journey, a journey that is taking me into the depths of grace where I am profoundly loved just as I am. No strings attached.

I guess my answer regarding home is not a literal place with a street address. My answer has its roots in some words from the Psalm 90, my favorite psalm, which I asked the minister to read at both of my parents' funerals.

The psalmist says God is our home. Wherever God is, we are at home. That's simply put and maybe more than enough. God is our home. We are in God's hands regardless.

Whether we live or die, we belong to God. That's grace.

May 19

We talk about our possessions, our this and that, but nothing really belongs to us. It all belongs to God, even the breath we breathe, and maybe we can just rest in that deep and quiet assurance.

Grace is the blessed assurance that we belong to God.

May 20

Sometimes I hold in my hand the old *Primitive Baptist Hymnal* that Grandmother Blake sang from and ultimately gave to me.

She told me one day her favorite hymn was Hymn 109, with these words at the end –

"Then millions of ages my soul would employ
In praising my Jesus, my love and my joy,
Without interruption, when all the glad throng,
With pleasures unceasing unite in the song."

Grace is singing songs of praise.

May 21

There was only one lone beautiful symbol left of my childhood when I went back to the home place where my grandparents lived. It was the old swing on the front porch.

It's the swing where my grandmother and I sat in the early evening just at dusk and listened to the whip-poor-wills as they sang their melodious songs from somewhere in the deep woods. Maybe that's the moment where my love of birds was born.

As far as I know, we don't have whip-poor-wills in these parts, and it's a pity. The last one I heard was at the farm of friends in southwest Georgia.

I still hear my Mama Blake saying, "Listen! Ain't that the prettiest music you ever heard?"

It was and still is the prettiest music I ever heard, and maybe that's home.

May 22

But you know, I am not finished with home quite yet.

There were also Tyler and Minnie Traylor, my maternal grandparents.

If the Blakes were the good country folk, the Traylors were the modest city slickers; in fact, for most all the years I knew them, they lived on Queenstown Avenue in Birmingham, Alabama.

My grandmother was a lovely, regal lady, prim and proper, her white finger-waved hair pulled back in curls. My grandfather was the quintessential gentleman, as kind and tender-hearted as any man I ever knew.

When my children asked me what I would like to be called by my grandchildren, I chose Granddaddy, which was the name we called my grandfather. Though I never rose to his level of goodness, I am glad the name we called him is being carried on by my grandchildren. It gives me something to aspire to, to hope for in my own journey.

Their home on Queenstown Avenue was small but very nicely kept.

I would go there in the summers, and my grandfather would sometimes take me to work with him. He was a plumbing inspector for the city, and in my little boy mind, I thought he must be important as all the plumbers paid attention to his recommendations when he spoke with them. He was a quiet, peaceful, loving man and, in some ways, always taking the backseat to my grandmother, who was a kind of matriarch for the family.

Grandparents are grace.

May 23

Grandmother Traylor was a wonderful cook, but I imagine just about all grandchildren think that about their grandmothers. I remember breakfast at her home when there were always fresh stewed prunes and poached eggs; "good for us," she said.

She had an old Underwood typewriter where she worked. I was never sure exactly what she was typing, but I can still see her now as she sat proudly at her desk. I can still hear her pecking away and the pauses before she dashed off again. Perhaps she was journaling and way ahead of her time. She also was a seamstress, always there to darn any sock, sew any pocket, and mend any tare in a shirt or pair of pants.

I remember when my grandparents' health began to fall apart, and it was decided that they must move into a nursing home. I can still feel their hearts breaking, but it was comforting that they were able to continue living together in the same room until my grandfather breathed his last breath.

Their fiftieth wedding anniversary was one of the happiest days, particularly of my grandmother's life. She beamed with joy and utter pride in her beloved Tyler. She was insistent that the whole family be present, and of course, we were all there. My grandparents lived a true love story; though it was a different time, back when things got broken, people fixed them rather than throwing them out like so much rubbish.

Christmas Day was the most festival day of the year. We would gather on Queenstown Avenue, and Grandmother would have the house decked out to the gills. There were three red bells on the front door that lit up one after the other. There was a magnificent silver tree in the window. There were small gifts for everybody. And oh my, there was ambrosia and Grandmother's coconut cake with the freshest coconut grated the day before. Her table was fit for kings and queens. Royalty.

Grace is a freshly baked coconut cake.

May 24

"For I know the plans I have for you,
declares the Lord.
Plans to prosper you and not to harm you.
Plans to give you hope and a future."

Jeremiah 29:11

May 25

*I go to nature to be soothed and healed,
and to have my senses put in order.*
—John Burroughs

Some mornings I am up and out long before dawn.

I long to observe the darkness. Venus, the bright and morning star, hanging like joy in the distance. A half-moon rendering just a hint of illumination, enough to bring a touch of invigoration to the night.

A sweet, cool, and refreshing light breeze sweeping across my warm face and my bare arms. The faint fragrance of honeysuckle in bloom reminds me of my roots in the Deep South and how much I embrace this geography of the heart.

There is often immense silence, an overflowing abundance of solitude, enough to easily breathe in and out, to cleanse my soul of the trappings that so easily beset the journey.

It seems like prayer.

Silence used to appear as an enemy, but now, now quietness is my traveling companion.

Thoreau said most men live lives of quiet desperation. There is no desperation in this kind of night, only a calm centering and a being still and knowing the oneness of all creatures great and small and that somehow the universe is intricately woven into the whole of this altogether brief and fleeting journey.

I wait in the dark night until I begin to hear birdsong just at dawn.

It is perhaps the greatest symphony I ever heard, filling the whole earth with gladness.

All over the woods, the morning dawns. Nature is aflame with the anticipation of another day to be awake in the infinite possibilities of life.

May 26

As I write these words before dawn, the thought of Anselm Atkins in his book *Nature Through a Lens Brightly* resonates with my journey: "The love of birds is a wide thing—yet itself a small thing in a wider love of nature, which is just another way of loving life."

Atkins chronicled a three-year personal account of living close to nature and savoring it, in simple, profound ways. He received his PhD in literature and theology from Emory University and died all too young in his early fifties of cancer.

I would have liked to have known this man.

I'd say nature, particularly getting to know the birds of the air, has been my great passion since retirement.

I have always had a love of nature and a curiosity for birds, but when I realized I didn't know their names or their ways, I decided it was time to do something about it. I remember the precise moment and place when I got permanently hooked on birds. It was the last day of December 2013, in the late afternoon at Turner Lake in Covington, Georgia, where I observed a small blue heron for a long time. Such beauty. Such grace.

Now I go everywhere I can to see what I can see, and my, oh my, the moments, like just yesterday when that Carolina Chickadee came around very quietly, and the mourning doves arrived, or a multitude of American goldfinches, magnificent in their bright lemon colors, came calling, or the red-bellied woodpecker made several appearances in his flight described as "undulating" because of his flaps in spurts. And there were the house finches, male and female, the northern cardinals just at dusk, and the big black American crow that came in for a landing. My heart goes off skipping a beat at the sight of them all.

May 27

My daughter tells me that when my seven-year-old grandson—who is already a lover of nature and says he wants to be an entomologist when he grows up—sees a bird, he exclaims, "Granddaddy would love that bird!"

He and I must go bird-watching again very soon, and don't you think that would be a good legacy to leave a grandchild?

It is easy for me to let stuff disturb my equilibrium. Nature is the place where I am most at home and where the noise and distractions of the journey give way to peace and solitude.

The words of Gretel Ehrlich come to mind: "Everything in nature invites us constantly to be what we are."

We understand, don't we? And we understand John Muir when he says, "When we are in nature, we are awake."

The grace of nature is the great awakening.

May 28

Bed of Leaves

I shall lie down in leaves
the shade of crimson
filled with abandonment,
wonder like a child
gazing into the distant sky.
Stretching my imagination
beyond where I can fly.
This bed of leaves
enticing, alluring,
full of fire.
I, an old man,
grown cold and tired.
I, an old man,
suddenly alive.

May 29

The God of the dirt
came up to me many times and said
so many wise and delectable things.
-Mary Oliver

I have so enjoyed my garden. It is at once therapeutic and healing, full of greenness and growth, of solace and surprises, of weeds and wonder.

To plant a seed in the ground, to sense that under the dirt and in the dark, the seed will fracture and sprout, is quite a delight. It is the stuff of life and is one of the great lessons the earth gives us for the journey.

I am fascinated by the way the stories in the Bible begin. I think it is no accident that the story begins in a garden.

It was during the exile when Israel had lost everything. The people had nothing but time on their hands, and so they told stories. They became a people of a book of stories in exile and certainly their take on Creation was quite a sweep of imaginative awe.

I care not a whit about the literalness of the story. In fact, I am, like most of us, a believer in evolution, not creationism, but the story is still quite beautiful, and it is a way of expressing the majesty, the mystery, and the transcendence of it all. Whoever did the editing wove the stories together, and we have this take on how it all came into being, and it was in a garden.

Spiritual or scientific? One myth or another one? What matters is that we are here. We are here for a brief moment in time, and how we spend our time in the garden makes all the difference in the world.

May 30

I am always moved when I hear a rendition of James Weldon Johnson's take on Creation ---

And God stepped out on space,
And He looked around and said,
"I'm lonely—
I'll make me a world."
And far as the eye of God could see
Darkness covered everything,
Blacker than a hundred midnights
Down in a cypress swamp.
Then God smiled,
And the light broke,
And the darkness rolled up on one side,
And the light stood standing on the other,
And God said, "That's good!"

And it was good and it is good, very good, and it is a garden.
I don't know what you grow in your garden. Since my space is limited, I grow tomatoes, squash, and cucumbers, peppers of all kinds, basil, cilantro, mint, and always sunflowers wherever there is a space to plant a seed.
Somehow it gives me hope and enlivens me for whatever life slings in my direction.
My garden keeps me low-down and close to the earth and forces me to bend down, kneel, and offer praise.
I think we can all create a garden wherever we are, wherever we live. We only need enough space to smell the earth and imagine the promise the sprouting brings.

June 1

One of my favorite books is a relatively new one, Paradise in Plain Sight: Lessons from a Zen Garden by Karen Miller, a Zen Buddhist priest who lives in Los Angeles. How I would like to sit at her feet and learn.

The book is not really about gardening so much as it is about living, about wakefulness in the everyday moments of life. Our moments are simple and ordinary, and the core of it is paying attention.

We miss so much in the hurry of our lives when maybe a garden teaches us to be still and wait and not to rush the seasons but to trust the seasons as they come and go.

A garden grows in silence, day by day. We plant, nurture, wait, and observe, and in due season, there is a harvest. First a bloom and then a tiny vegetable, and then a mature vegetable for our delight, and it is good, very good. I do not think it is so much the gardener's skills as it is sun and water, gifts given for the garden, and so it is with life itself and with this journey journey on Grace Street.

We need not run ahead. We can trust the process. We can wait.

I like what Miller does with weeds. She says, "Paradise is a patch of weeds." She thought of what she would do with the rest of her life and hit on a scheme, an enterprise. She would not be a landscape designer or a decorator. She would go to people's houses every week and just pull weeds not just once but over and over again, and she would ultimately get to the roots of the weeds.

Got any weeds in your garden? If you are like me, you surely do. Miller says this is how our lives become rich with purpose as we take care of things right under our feet, moment by moment, day by day.

June 2

The Teacher said, "Unless a grain of wheat falls into the ground and dies, it cannot live," and maybe that is the greatest lesson of the garden.

It is a law of nature. It is a fact of life. This dying is the only way to life, a fractured seed broken open and coming to the miracle of life.

Richard Rohr, a Franciscan priest of the New Mexico province, has profoundly influenced by life through his prolific writings. I go back to his words over and over again. He calls us from the false self to the true self. He calls us to a radical realignment of the false self to the true self through change, which does not come easily.

Like Thomas Merton, Rohr suggests that it is not the body that has to die but the false self that we do not need anyway.

This fractured seed may be an illness, like cancer or some other disease.

It may be a broken relationship. It may be some struggle that never seems to go away as it drives us to our knees with our backs to the wall, a thorn in the side, or some wearisome, troublesome valley through which we travel.

How the seed is fractured is not the important thing. The important thing is that the seed breaks open in the darkness and comes forth as something beautiful, something worthy, something that is very good, and that is part of why the garden out my window is such grace to my heart.

June 3

Look at the birds of the air; they do not
sow or reap or store away in barns,
and yet your heavenly Father feeds them. Are
you not much more valuable than they?
—Jesus

Frequently, and then sometimes extraordinarily, great blessing falls on us. Others may consider where blessing originates or precisely what happens in those moments, but you know it's true, don't you? You know those times beyond measure, comprehension, or ability to articulate. I think I'll just call them gift moments, which immensely enrich our journeys.

That's what happened to me in the woods the first time I went birdwatching with Frances Rowland, a remarkable woman who was married to Tom for sixty years.

The lovely couple let nature grow naturally and with more abundance around their old home place than I can express. They are flesh-and-blood testimonies to our oneness with creation, all creatures great and small. They just ring true, the salt of the earth.

Frances and Tom raised six sons on twenty-five acres of deep woodland and a big garden and a pond. Jody, one of their sons, died of AIDS at age thirty. He died in their arms at home in 1991, and Jody's brothers built a nature garden on the property with all indigenous plants and trees to memorialize their beloved brother.

That's a moving story, isn't it, of a family in rural Georgia, quietly and proudly loving their boy?

Grace is forever saying Yes to those we love.

June 4

Frances Rowland was an ornithologist, a very knowledgeable birder, and a great one at that.

She took me birding in her woodlands. I steadied her arm while she used her binoculars, and oh, the delight we shared one day. She reminisced about far-off places that Tom and she had gone just to see if they could observe a single species.

She was a bird-watcher for many years. What a time we had wandering through the woods. How many times did I hear her say, "Listen! Listen! Listen!" and we would listen to sweet birdsong, and she would say "That's a great-crested flycatcher" or "That's a pileated woodpecker" or "That's an eastern towhee."

I saw my first tufted titmouse, a common bird in these parts, while birding with Frances. I saw my first summer tanager, a brilliant red male, and imagine the joy Frances and I felt when she observed and she showed me my first scarlet tanager, a male with a red body and black wings. We observed for a long time as wrens, eastern bluebirds, and northern cardinals nested, males and females taking care of their young.

I took a beautiful photograph of the eastern bluebirds going in and out of their house as well as a tiny Northern Cardinal being born.

We sat for a while, surrounded by silence and birdsong and the sweet scent of honeysuckle in the spring down south. We reminisced about our experiences with whip-poor-wills.

We talked about the times when tears ran down our faces at the sight of the birds of the air. "Just wait till you see your first indigo bunting as they migrate," Frances said with anticipation, and "Oh, did I tell you there is a green heron on the pond?" And she said more than once, "Come back to see us anytime. I don't meet many people like you." Her spirit soared and I always had a sense she already had one foot in heaven.

June 5

I wrote about our initial visit and took what I had written to Frances as a gift.

When I shared my words with her about our visit, she said, "That's the prettiest thing I ever read about my family and me."

On that day, I took her a dozen copies of a picture I took of Frances with her binoculars. "What will I ever do with twelve pictures?" she asked.

I responded, "I imagine there are many among your family and friends who will want this picture of you."

I went to see her at least three times, and every time she said, "Why don't you stay a little longer?"

Frances was ill, and soon after I met her, she went to the hospital where she struggled and died.

She slipped away one day just before noon and went yonder, and I was sad though I only knew her for a very short time. I cannot begin to imagine what Tom, her husband, and her sons as well as others who knew her and loved her for so long must have felt. She left a mark of love on me for the rest of my life. She stirred my soul and I felt a strong connection with her soul, as if she'd always been a part of me.

I hear her now: "Just wait till you see your first indigo bunting."

I did Frances, I did, but I never got to tell you. Maybe Frances sent that beautiful bird to me to let me know that all was well with her soul and would be with mine when the time comes to go yonder.

June 6

They've all been here today.

A multitude of American Goldfinches, quite a number of house finches, a few northern cardinals, a couple of mourning doves, an assortment of sparrows, and the eastern bluebirds are back. The bluebirds keep going in and out of a birdhouse along the fence line where they are nesting. I can see them as I write.

Even the squirrels and chipmunks have been munching on Leftovers. A rather rip-roaring, frolicking good time is had by all.

The whole assembly left rather quickly in a moment and there was silence, and I saw a shadow flying across the ground and then a huge hawk landed on a pole and sat there a while like he was a king, bigger than all the other birds and critters.

And then, oh my, a ruby-throated hummingbird came to drink the nectar. In fact, the hummingbird drank from the feeder three times. Such a magnificent creature, darting quickly to drink and then flying away to the bushes.

I do not know precisely what Jesus meant when he said "Consider the birds of the air."

I think he meant "Pay attention. Pay attention to what is around you."

I think he meant "Look up. Look up."

June 7

    I keep with me most all the time some words of the poet e. e. Cummings, whose grave I visited one mellow autumn Sabbath in Boston ---

> *may my heart always be open to little*
> *birds who are the secrets of living*
> *whatever they sing is better than to know*
> *and if men should not hear them men are old.*

June 8

My imagination is a monastery and I am its monk.
—John Keats

The deepest expressions of my spiritual journey have been emerging from the Abbey of Gethsemani in Bardstown, Kentucky, and the Monastery of the Holy Spirit in Conyers, Georgia.

In fact, there is a rich connection between the two monasteries as brothers from Kentucky came to Georgia in 1944 to build the church with the sweat of their brows and the prayers of their hearts.

These holy places are an oasis for me, a well of living water in the midst of what sometimes is a desert.

I have had the great pleasure of spending time with a number of monks, some of whom have lived a life of monasticism for forty or fifty years and more. They have given themselves over to poverty, silence, celibacy.

We are witnessing the decline of some of the Western world's version of Christianity. Some of the Americanized version, including the "health, wealth and prosperity" mindset, was very detrimental to our spirituality.

Monasticism reminds us of the basics and what matters. Our souls are fed in silence and in waiting. I think of the words of Walt Whitman, the great American poet, as he speaks prophetically, "Re-examine all you have been told. Dismiss what insults your soul."

We are seeing the emergence of new expressions of spirituality that come to us from the East.

Scores of people long for meditation, quiet centering, and solitude.

June 9

So much so that we are told the spirituality of the twenty-first century will be characterized by the kinds of virtue that are apparent in monasticism.

Most of us are not called to a life as a hermit or to a community of faith such as a monastery, but I believe we are called to explore the silence, the natural order, the giving of ourselves over to quietude.

There are those who say that monasticism is an escape from the real world. Au contraire. There may be more reality in the quiet solitude of a community where people pray for the world than is found at the rising and falling of the New York Stock Exchange.

There may be more reality in a monastery than in the illusionary world of what we consider to be power, success and status. There may be more reality in chanting the ancient psalms than in reading our horoscopes. We are after reality or bedrock, not transient illusion.

June 10

I remember the monks I have encountered at the Abbey of Gethsemani where Thomas Merton lived until his early death while speaking in Thailand.

I think of Brothers Conrad, Christian, Frederick, and Paul.

Brother Conrad, age eighty-five, has been at the monastery for fifty-six years. His boyhood years were spent on a farm in Owensboro, Kentucky. He is a joyful, happy man. He takes me on a little tour of the cloistered area and shares and signs his book *Monastic Reflections*. We agree to correspond. He says if he had his life to live over again, he would "do it all over again tomorrow."

He says, "Grace occurs in unexpected places and times—like our meeting today."

Interesting how in providence two people meet and something of the supernatural, the mystical occurs, and there is this wonderful connection, a grace moment. It is always good. It is always a surprising gift.

Brother Christian is the current guest master at Gethsemani. He is a birder and an accomplished—actually, magnificent—photographer. He shows me a number of his photographs, and he is especially pleased to share the birds he has observed. I wish for more time to have a conversation. Maybe again someday.

June 11

Brother Frederick, now ninety-four, originally from Kansas City, is the oldest monk at Gethsemani. He has been at the monastery for sixty years, except for three years when he served in Chili.

He was led to the monastic life by reading Thomas Merton's *The Seven Storey Mountain* and was at the abbey for ten years with Merton, whom he says was "the best teacher I ever had, a cosmopolitan person, a kind of a romantic but very human."

Frederick says he is meditating on death more than usual because of his age, and "Death reminds me to live today."

When a monk dies, two brothers sit on either side of their departed brother and alternate reading the Psalms for twenty-four hours prior to the burial.

Of grace, Frederick says, "That's the whole story. God working in us. We all need plenty of help."

Brother Paul is a poet, the author of several published books. He has been at the monastery for more than fifty years. We talk of writing and his favorite poets, and he says he writes one haiku every day. When we were at Merton's Hermitage at Gethsemani, Paul read an entry out loud from Merton's journal dated April 23, 1961, and it was so very moving.

June 12

I got to have a conversation with Brother Matthew Kelty a few times before he died at Gethsemani, and I stopped by his grave the other day on the burial ground where the monks are laid to rest.

I recall what Matthew said: "The healing of the world does not begin in some far-off land that we must hasten to help, but in the geography of your own heart. There the sinner is washed in mercy and becomes thereby an instrument of mercy, not merely by his prayers, but in everything he does. For he is a vessel of grace. We cannot heal all the world's problems, but we begin with our own heart if our help is to amount to anything."

All grace comes by way of the heart, and it is never contrived. We are those open vessels. We are the instruments of grace. We are the healing balm of Gilead.

June 13

At the Monastery of the Holy Spirit near my home, I have had extraordinary conversations with a number of the monks. We have talked of grace and mortality and a life given over to solitude and silence. The monks seem so very human as they breathe the natural air and are at one with God and creation.

I recently stood at the grave of Brother Luke, a founder of the monastery in Conyers who came from Kentucky. Luke began his monastic journey when he was a young man at the age of twenty-one, and he was a monk for eighty-one years. He lived a hidden life of prayer, solitude, community, and oneness with creation.

The last time I saw Luke, he was one hundred and one years of age. He was making prayer beads, and he was as joyful and peaceful as any man I ever encountered.

The little monk with dancing eyes quipped, "This is the last work station of the monk prior to his death."

A year later, he died.

June 14

I pull from the shelves of my books an old book I have
treasured for many years. It is The Broken Body by Jean Vanier.
Vanier was the founder of the worldwide L'Arche communities
and Faith and Light communities for people with mental
disabilities.

Though not monastic, many of the expressions of
monasticism are found in these communities. It was the
cause for which Henri Nouwen gave the last years of his life.

Vanier writes,

"Love not just those of your own tribe,
your own class, family or people,
but those who are different,
those who are strangers,
who are strange to your ways,
who come from different cultural and religious traditions,
who seem odd,
Those you do not understand."

Grace is loving people of other tribes.

June 15

After a number of prominent artists in the Atlanta area spent a week at the monastery, their art was on display in a gallery and was offered for the benefit of the monastery. What an amazing collection of art, maybe fifty pieces and more.

I was particularly drawn to the art of Margaret Dyer and a piece she called *Morning Vigils*. It is an oil, 11 × 14 and beautifully framed. The painting now has a prominent place in my home.

When I first saw the piece, I was moved by the solemnity of it, particularly after being told that the artist painted her work essentially in the dark. There was just very faint light in the monastery church while the monks were singing as she painted.

"Painting in the dark," a monk said to me, and I thought of Barbara Brown Taylor's book *Learning to Walk in the Dark*.

Painting, walking, living sometimes in the dark, we go on.

But you say, you like light more than darkness, and I understand more than you could possibly know; however, we live part of the journey in darkness, mystery, the unknown and the unanswered, the perplexing questions of life.

June 16

I am trying to rid myself of the old dualism by which I lived for so long. I will not write of darkness versus light, for they are both one and the same. You only have to read whoever wrote the Old Testament narrative culminating in Exodus 19 to find the writer saying that God was in a dark cloud.

God is light. God is darkness.

I called Margaret Dyer, the painter of *Morning Vigils*, on the telephone, and we had a lovely conversation.

She said she woke at the 4:00 a.m. bell, grabbed her paint and easel, and rushed to the back of the church. She was struck by the darkness and solemnity of the moment as she heard the monks as they sang.

"I was not necessarily moved by the spirituality of the moment but stunned by the visual."

Margaret Dyer said she heard the monks singing five times a day and that, when she went back to her home, she could still hear them singing.

I hear the monks singing too in this work of art I now see every day.

June 17

I take refuge in the woods, the ones surrounding the monastery once or often twice a week, sometimes more. I am like a sponge as I am just back from my recent days of surgery and recuperation.

The trees are full of birdsong; the birds of the air remind me of what the Teacher said about concentrating on these beautiful creatures and also what he said on another occasion about giving attention to the little children.

They are, you know, more one and the same, as we are all one, than we could possibly imagine.

There is a faint fragrance of honeysuckle in the deeper woods, and the magnolias are more beautiful than I ever remember.

June 18

Since it is early morning, there is a cool breeze, a healing peace.

I meet Joe, a young man out of Atlanta who is on a personal retreat.

"You Catholic?" I inquire.

"No, my wife is. I am just a seeker," he answers.

I whisper back, "Me too, a seeker."

Earlier in the day, a stranger, but perhaps there are no strangers with whom we cross paths, writes me out of nowhere in social media to tell me she has read something I wrote.

She says, "Random stopping by. While I am in no way spiritual, your entry reminds me to give pause and thanks for the things in my life that keep me above water."

We understand, don't we? Seekers, in whatever way we choose to describe or define ourselves, staying above water, travelers together on the journey, really less different from each other than we suspect.

June 19

I meet Brother Callistus by chance at a fork in the road. He observes, "You look like you're lost."

"No," I laugh, "I'm found."

He is from Trinidad, and he has been at the monastery for twenty-five years.

I ask if his name is one he took when he became a monk as is frequently the custom, and he says that Callistus is in fact his given name, though there was a pope named Callixtus in the third century.

We talk a while and there is an instant association. I ask him to tell me about grace, and he laughs and says we need three days to talk about it before he zeros in with these words: "Grace is God's never-ending outpouring of God's being as gift to us."

He gives me a gift of grace: "Anytime you would like, come sit alongside us monks in the choir stalls and sing with us."

Grace is singing with the monks and the birds of the air.

June 20

And there was Thomas with whom there was instant rapport.

You know, that kind of intimacy you just naturally flow into with a fellow traveler with whom you have never spent time, yet you sense the heart of the other.

Thomas is eighty-six and has been at the monastery for sixty-two years. He is about as awake and alive as anyone I have encountered.

We talk of Thomas Merton, whom Thomas referred to as "no-plaster-of-paris saint," altogether human, angry at times. And isn't there plenty to be angry about in our world?

We discuss the difference between communion and communication and decry the "superficial communication" of our day. So many ways to communicate, you name them, yet they are often superficial.

We consider prayer as communion, not communication, not our talking but our getting quiet long enough to listen.

We, of course, talk of grace, which my new friend refers to as "the ability to grow in love."

He tells me, "Grace is the most abused word in our circles as if it was some kind of precious liquid."

He speaks of grace as living in the presence of God and each other, and he says, "There are no ungraced moments. Everything is grace."

He intones, "Grace is to be loved unconditionally and irreversibly," and questions, "What more do you want, mister?" I answer, "Nothing really, mister, nothing!" as my heart begins to sing out loud.

Not grace plus. Grace period. Grace alone.

We embrace as we part company, and he whispers, "Peace and love, brother."

I say, "You're a grace-filled man."

He responds, "I'm just mirroring you, mister."

June 21

None of us doubt for a single moment, the joy that children are. So fresh from the Creator, they are the greatest vessels of grace in our lives.

They are our teachers and our mentors, and we would do well to simply allow them to lead us.

Grandson Adam asks, "You know what I want to be when I grow up, Mama?"

"What, son?"

"I want to be a comedian."

"Why a comedian?"

"So I can make people laugh."

A right, fine calling, I'd say.

Grace is laughter, deep-belly laughter.

June 22

Granddaughter Marlie Grace, the oldest of my grandchildren, expresses admiration for a woman in her life that is on her way to Ethiopia with the Peace Corps in these words: "I think you are extremely, incredibly brave and selfless for volunteering your time to help children in need."

Grace is offering a helping hand to people in need.

June 23

Granddaughter Claire went off to camp and was away from home for several nights.

Her mama asked, "Are you nervous at all about spending four whole nights away from home at camp?"

"No," comes Claire's flat and matter-of-fact response.

Her mama said, "Wow. You're awesome."

Claire said, "Yeah. I get that a lot."

I am glad Claire gets that. I hope we all do.

Grace is knowing we are awesome.

June 24

Five-year-old great-nephew Brody and I are having a conversation on Easter Sunday at his home.

He sees bumblebees in his yard and questions whether he should venture out until he says, "Sometimes you just have to face your fears head-on."

Grace is facing our fears head-on.

June 25

Grandson Elijah is my bird-watching companion when I am in Kentucky.

Imagine his delight and mine when he first spots a red-winged blackbird. "Look, Granddaddy!" he exclaims.

I ask Elijah, "What do you think of life?"

"I like it!" he says.

Grace is liking this magnificent life we are given.

June 26

I send a little gift to each of the families of my three children.

The plaque reads, "In this place / We do love / We do laughter/ We do encouragement / We do mistakes / We do forgiveness / We do grace."

Grandson Owen says, "I love that gift that Granddaddy gave us. It looks very beautiful and important."

He's the grandson who was asked why he likes to wear Band-Aids even if he doesn't have a scratch or a particular need for one. His answer: "Band-Aids make me happy."

Grace is a Band-Aid that makes us happy.

June 27

I hear a little boy over the fence in my neighborhood, not more than two or three years of age, as he says to his father or maybe grandfather, "I lead. I lead. You follow. You follow."

I thrill to a parade of two characters, one a little boy and the other an aging man. And so it is as the little children lead us.

Grace -- the children who lead us.

June 28

I think there's just one kind of folks. Folks.
—Harper Lee, **To Kill a Mockingbird**

I went again recently to the Civil Rights Memorial in Montgomery, Alabama, the heart of the Old South, in the shadow of the state capital and not far from the Dexter Avenue Baptist Church where the young preacher Martin Luther King began the revolution.

The memorial is a stark reminder of the price paid for the freedom of all people. There are the names of forty people who died in the struggle.

They are immortalized by Maya Lin, the Chinese-American sculptor who also designed the Vietnam Memorial in Washington.

I put my hand in the water at the memorial in a moment of remembrance.

I am drawn to the memorial as I am drawn to all those sacred places of civil rights history, like Montgomery, Selma, Birmingham, Atlanta, and Memphis. Many times I have stood on the holy ground in those places to remember and never forget. We must never forget and we must teach the stories of what happened in those places to succeeding generations.

In Montgomery, I visited the Southern Poverty Law Center, founded by Morris Dees, author of a moving autobiography of his advocacy of human rights. I send a small contribution whenever I can to the ongoing work of justice and equality for all people.

We will not forget Rosa Parks, a woman of courage and faith who refused to sit in the back of the bus. We keep up the struggle until we are all free and, as is said, "Until justice rolls down like water and righteousness like a mighty stream."

June 29

When I was a boy, my parents took me to the first inauguration of George Wallace, the fiery governor of Alabama

I heard him say those flawed and misguided words: "Segregation today. Segregation tomorrow. Segregation forever."

Years later I met the speech writer who gave Wallace his words, and he sent me away from his presence, saying, "I see we have a different point of view and nothing in common," and he was right.

Would to God that we may learn to follow the African proverb "In times of crisis, the foolish build dams while the wise build bridges.

Grace is about building bridges.

June 30

These bridges of which I write include every arena of civil rights, based on the profound dignity and worth of all people.

We are not home yet when it comes to the civil rights of all races, nor are we home yet regarding the role of women, particularly in the Roman Catholic Church, nor are we home yet when it comes to immigration, nor are we home yet when it comes to the rights of two people who love each other to live together in marriage and enjoy all the rights and privileges and responsibilities of everybody else.

Partly because I am a gay man, I have a particular passion to see this last great bastion of inequality broken to pieces and removed from the landscape of our society.

I affirm the words of John Lewis, civil rights icon and US congressperson from Atlanta, who says, "I fought too long and too hard against discrimination based on race and color, not to stand up and fight against discrimination based on sexual orientation."

July 1

I have only come face to face with one archbishop of Canterbury, the head of the Church of England and the symbolic head of the worldwide Anglican Communion.

His name is George Carey and he was at the time of our encounter an emeritus archbishop. I had an exchange with him and found him to be quite unlike Emeritus Archbishop Rowan Williams who led the Anglican Church through deep and troubled waters, with much travail, over the issue of human sexuality and to a wider place of spirituality.

The setting with George Carey was a large downtown Episcopal Church in Memphis. It was a weeknight during Lent.

The archbishop's topic was the subject of homosexuality and particularly the ordination of gays in the church.

When it came time for questions, I went to the microphone and posed a very simple question: "Archbishop Carey, sir, I would like to ask you to flesh out a bit of why you are opposed to homosexuality and to the current direction of the Anglican Church?"

His answer in full was "Because the Bible says so."

I thought I was hearing some conservative from Tulsa or Toledo or Montgomery or Milwaukee who had never grappled with the issues in any deep or profound way or given himself over to the light dawning as we are led into a new day.

People may different on this important topic, but I was shocked by Carey's words.

Grace is about not only a proper understanding of Scripture but reason, tradition, and experience as the ways we approach the living out of our lives.

July 2

Recently, I stumbled in and then quickly out of a conversation that I originally thought would at least be some dialogue, even if there was no particular bearing with one other, with some conservative fellows on the subject at hand.

I affirmed with them that I am a gay man. I affirmed that I am a progressive, a liberal, and thus speak from a certain perspective. I also said all of us have this treasure in earthen vessels, left and right, and see through a glass darkly.

These fellows all have conservative credentials. They point to the progressives for causing trouble in "their" church. One used an obviously biased sixteen-year-old article from another conservative to suggest they were right on the subject.

Certain ideas exist and have merit always in conversation, but I wanted to know what new thought the writer has had since he had written that he was open to conversation sixteen years ago. What real conversation has the professor had with people of a differing perspective since he wrote his article?

There was no response. A good part of the spiritual world has long since moved on, and some people are still stuck in an absurd quagmire over what may well be a nonissue when the big issues continue to be with us: racism, greed, violence, poverty, and the list goes on.

Grace is openness to a divergence of thought.

July 3

This conservative mind-set has a single track. A couple of these fellows say that culture has overtaken "their" church, and I suggested perhaps culture may indeed have something to say to segments of the institutional church where there is laziness and slothfulness and a need for serious grappling with the issues.

I honestly observe them as being married to a certain culture themselves. They do not have any real answers except to repeat what they have swallowed and mouthed all these years.

In fact, those men are mostly silent, never giving credence to the fact that I too have a voice and a belief system and a way of seeing things. Sadly, it seems they will live and die in a splintered, divided church with no hope of reconciliation instead of bearing with and living with people who see things quite differently than they do.

I believe we are missing so much, so very much, when we put all our eggs in one basket, put all our stakes down in one place, and do not embrace the whole story, all of it, where reason, experience, and the written guide exist as a three-legged stool to discern what is right and just.

The saddest thing is that young people and others are caught in the middle, struggling with their sexuality, trying desperately to understand themselves and the world around them while those who are called to lead hunker down like scared rabbits in political and theological camps of self-righteousness.

Oh, the arrogance by which we sometimes live.

July 4

How could we be so presumptuous as to think any one of us speaks for God alone or that we do not need each other to discern what is merciful, just, and gracious, welcoming of all people?

No wonder good people of an alternative lifestyle like me simply ignore segments of the institutional church. No wonder many leave the institutional church and find a deeper spirituality elsewhere.

I knew a long time ago where I stood with God as a gay man, and I refuse to let anyone separate me from God.

Segments of the church got it wrong on race and on the role of women and in so many other areas. Why?

Because they say, "The Bible says so."

The wind of the Spirit is moving on, and we would do well to follow where the Spirit leads in a new day of grace, grace and mercy and peace and love for all people. It's Grace Street.

I share the belief of those who say, if we could turn down the rhetoric and stop arguing about things that do not matter and rid ourselves of our pride, we might just discover that our singular contribution to these difficult times is community.

Not just niceness, smiles, and positive thinking but radically open and transformative community. We are to be one not always right. We are to love one another not judge one another.

July 5

Certainly one of the most moving moments of my life was a pilgrimage to Hayneville, Alabama.

It's the place where Jonathan Daniels, Caucasian, age twenty-six, a native of Keene, New Hampshire, the Valedictorian of his class at Virginia Military Institute, a seminarian studying at Cambridge, spending the summer helping poor Blacks in Alabama, was gunned down and killed instantly by a murderer, Caucasian, who used a 12-gauge shotgun to fulfill his evil intent.

All because Jonathan Daniels and a small mixed crowd wanted to buy a soda in a local grocery store on that fateful day in 1965.

It has been a long journey and it was never just a regional southern conflict. It was always about the soul of the nation because isn't it true that bigotry, discrimination, hatred, people fighting people have no geographic boundaries?

Isn't it true that the Edmund Pettus Bridge in Selma, near Hayneville, is one of the most sacred places on earth and the key to the freedom of all people everywhere?

You only have to hear the story of a mountain under siege in Iraq to know the universality of the struggle. You only have to see the scene of an ugly-spirited crowd in southern California as they fight the immigration of people from across the border, to understand that it was never about the south alone. It was and is always about the human family around the world.

July 6

Jonathan Daniels -- His name is known around the world by people who know their history including their civil rights history. Jonathan Daniels, recognized as a martyr by the Episcopal Church and the worldwide Anglican community.

Jonathan Daniels, who pushed Ruby Sales, a young Black girl, out of the way and took the fatal bullet.

It was Ruby Sales who said, "Where there is no memory, there can be no hope."

We would just as soon forget, wouldn't we? We try often in our arrogant ways. We try to erase it all from our memory and let our children and our grandchildren carry on the same old bigotry, the same old prejudice, the same old injustice. Let us legalize it, build our political allegiances around it. Let us wrap our warped and perverted views of the Bible around it. Or so we think in our ignorance.

Those outside Northern agitators were disturbing our peaceful way of living. Why didn't they all just go home and leave us alone? We'll take care of things, but it takes some time, a hundred years and more is not long enough and Martin Luther King thunders back the truth: we can't wait any longer.

But we can't forget, can we? And it is still in our memory isn't it? We must never forget. We must keep telling the story over and over again if there is any hope for us. We must tell the story to our children, our grandchildren, to each succeeding generation.

We must write a profoundly new narrative and be vigilant every day in a time when the old ways are creeping back into our social and political discourse.

July 7

A lot of us, surrounded by a great cloud of witnesses, are on a contrary journey and will keep swimming against the currents until justice is done.

In Hayneville, Alabama, I marched with a couple of hundred people. We sang the old songs of the movement. We stopped at the jail where the agitators were kept in deplorable conditions.

We shared the Sacrament of Holy Communion in the old courthouse where the murderer of Jonathan Daniels was acquitted by an all-white jury.

We got on our knees at the sacred spot where Jonathan Daniels' blood spilled on to the hard, cold concrete and where he died.

It was Daniels himself who wrote these profound words shortly before his death, "The doctrines of the creeds, the enacted faith of the sacraments, were the essential preconditions of the experience itself.

The faith with which I went to Selma has not changed: it has grown . . . I began to know in my bones and sinews that I had been truly baptized into the Lord's death and resurrection . . . with them, the black and white men, with all life, in him whose Name is above all names that the races and nations shout . . .we are indelibly and unspeakably one."

July 8

I remember traveling back from Hayneville, on the road from Selma to Montgomery.

I was exhausted, dripping in the sweat of the day, weary from the battle with my health of recent months, but in my heart I was at peace with the journey I have lived. I felt grateful for the opportunities I have had and for whatever small voice I have offered when it comes to the dignity and civil rights of all people.

I wondered if I have made any difference. I certainly did not pay the ultimate sacrifice that Jonathan Daniels paid. I wondered if my children, and their children, would carry on the message when I am gone.

The day Jonathan Daniels gave the Valedictorian address at VMI, he closed with these words, "I wish you the joy of a purposeful life." That is the way to move from the old narrative to the new narrative and the only way that will change the world.

Grace is a new narrative and a purposeful life.

Listen with the ear of your heart.

St. Benedict

July 10

By your grace I am here.
-Franz Wright

We keep digging at the truth, trying to articulate what grace is. We know there are some simple and profound answers that come to us from sacred texts and by the word of those who have experienced grace.

About as close as I can come to describing grace, for me at least, is to tell you a story. I hesitate to share it because it was at once mystical and very real and there have been very few moments, if any other moments, exactly like this, for me.

I was sitting in a nondescript room just before evening came.

I was not thinking of anything in particular, certainly not focused on spiritual thoughts of any kind, when it seemed like, out of nowhere, a great wave of love came over me. It was like wave after wave of love crashing to the shore of my heart and flooding me for no apparent reason.

I know there was nothing I had done to anticipate the moment. It was more than my poor heart could take, and I finally said to the nothingness of the space or to whatever presence there was, "Stop! I can take no more of this love. It is overwhelming me."

It was not an experience that lasted even thirty minutes, and I did not feel changed in a tangible way. Whatever happened was more the deep and profound awareness that I was accepted just as I was and that love, *agape* love, was everywhere.

July 11

Ed Nelson of Georgia is man I love like a brother.

I call him a renegade in the best sense of the word. He simply listens to the beat of a different drummer, and it is no accident that, when he was a younger man, he took his place in the crowd behind the coffin of Martin Luther King as it was carried along the streets of Atlanta, Georgia.

He says, "I am not sure that I have ever lived via sola grace. The risk is too great. Most of us talk a good line about it."

Truth be told, Ed lives grace. "I have long believed in universal redemption. I don't believe a tiny speck of stardust [radiated carbon] or a genetic divine spark, *pneuma* [spirit] or soul [*psyche*] is wasted or lost. The 'best,' whatever that is, is yet to be. I believe in Eternal Being."

Ed presses, "I want to see or hear about your lashes up the Via Dolorosa, the awful pain and burden of the crossbar, nail prints in your hands or wrists, hole in your side."

I tell Ed, "That's not my experience, and as far as I know, if the narrative is true, there is only One who walked that path."

July 12

How easy to frustrate the grace of God. I think of the words of Thomas Merton in his Journal dated April 7, 1941: "I am like a man, a thief and a murderer, put in jail and condemned for stealing and murdering all my life, for murdering God's grace in myself and others."

Such powerfully convicting words. Let us not be guilty of disturbing God's grace in ourselves or others.

Through grace and grace alone, I and the whole human family of people on earth are the recipients of what Jesus did. It is mystery and beyond my comprehension. There is absolutely nothing I can do to earn it or deserve it or to merit such amazing love.

Grace says that there is nothing we could ever do that would make God love us less or more. Whatever failures or weaknesses any of us have are absolutely irrelevant in the face of such all-pervading grace.

But you say you don't believe a word of any of this. You say it is all a fabricated story, and I say you may be right and I may be wrong, but what if it is true?

Is Jesus the only way to God? I do not think so. There are many paths to God and many great religions and spiritualities to explore, but Jesus is one of the ways and Jesus is a path I have chosen.

Maybe you have to get naked, stripped of all the trappings of the false self, to ever begin to imagine grace. There are no clean elegant robes of respectability and good works in this nakedness.

That is the heart of the matter when it comes to grace with as much clarity as I can give it.

July 13

Frederick Buechner grapples with it: "The grace of God means something like: Here is your life. You might never have been, but you are because the party wouldn't have been complete without you."

Grace is not a concept, not an abstract, not an "it" or a mushy melted marshmallow.

Grace chases, goes where grace is not supposed to go, doesn't follow the rules, but with wild abandonment and boundless energy, pursues us like a lover in the night. We just get on board and realize we are not in the driver's seat.

Grace is not an excuse for a sloppy life. It's the power to overcome a wasted life, for there is a cost involved in coming to our true selves, our ultimate authenticity, and after this grace gets way down deep in the marrow of our being, we may accomplish our one singular mission to love.

July 14

There are these profound words of Richard Rohr, founder and director of the Center of Action and Contemplation in Albuquerque, New Mexico, which are found in his book *Eager to Love*:

"Grace is inherent to creation from the beginning and not a later add-on, or a dole-out to the worthy or the churched, or a prize for the perfect. This completely rearranges the spiritual universe most of us were educated into, where grace was an add-on, an occasional filling of the gaps, a churchy thing, a prize for the perfect, and even then, only now and then."

Any of us interested in revolutionizing our lives would do well to grab hold of those words by Rohr which are at the heart of spirituality.

July 15

I am always in the company of great books and would consider my life shallow and lacking in meaning if it were not for the books that have changed and actually saved my life.

When it comes to traveling on Grace Street, I am indebted to Charles H. Spurgeon's classic *All of Grace* and Frederick Buechner's *The Alphabet of Grace.* I am grateful for Simone Weil's *Gravity and Grace.* I am enlightened and find hope in Kathleen Dowling Singh's *The Grace of Dying* and *The Grace of Aging* and *The Grace of Living.* Singh works with dying patients in a large hospice in southwestern Florida and has extensive experience and training in transpersonal psychology and various spiritual traditions. I find help in other contemporary writings on grace such as Ken Wilber's *Grace and Grit,* Miroslav Volf's *Free of Charge,* Philip Yancey's *What's So Amazing about Grace,* Max Lucado's *Grace: More than We Deserve, Greater than We Imagine,* and two of Tullian Tchividjian's books, *Surprised by Grace:God's Relentless Pursuit of Rebels* and *One Way Love: Inexhaustible Grace for an Exhausted World.*

There is a wealth of grace in reading books that stir the soul.

July 16

Allen Pruitt, rector of Saint Mark's Episcopal Church in LaGrange, Georgia, has been a great mentor for me in the school of grace.

I like what he has to say about the rhythm of God's grace,

"There is a rhythm to everything. There is a rhythm to the work of Almighty God. God's rhythm is not fitful or broken. God's rhythm is grace. Our rhythm is so often broken. Wars and rumors of wars; planes shot out of the sky; girls stolen by lunatic armies. These are not natural disasters, not plagues brought on by the physical world. These are horrors within our control. These are horrors that are all too human. Our rhythm is a broken one, lurching from one step to the next, lost, even when we might have been found. The rhythm of evil is insidious: lurking, infiltrating until it finally destroys. God's ways are very different. God never seeks destruction, even the destruction of evil, neither through overwhelming force nor by cunning tricks. Instead, God seeks only to redeem evil. God seeks to find that which has died and to bring it to new life. What rhythm have you found in your own life? Is that rhythm calling you toward life or death, toward destruction or grace? Can you hear God's rhythm in the silence of your rest? Can you hear it above the din and confusion of your busy life? We see more than we deserve; we are promised more than we could ever earn. Because that is grace; because that is God's rhythm whether we can hear it or not."

July 17

Interesting to me, at least, that I can almost trace the origin of the seed that was planted as to grace that comes to us in our struggle to liberation.

It was forty years ago, and I see how at every step of the way the thought of grace has been unfolding in my journey and how today grace sustains me.

People say, "You don't have to be strong all the time," and the truth is, I am not.

Sometimes I tremble. Sometimes I cry, but I know this: in my weakness, grace takes over and I am carried on the wings of the morning and the night, and that's no empty or shallow cliché.

It is, in fact, the experience through which I am traveling not of myself or by myself but of God, who sustains me. It causes me to be grateful and to praise and to say glory. Bravado? Of course not. How absurd would that be?

July 18

This thought of grace originated in my reading of the *Collected Stories of Flannery O'Connor*, which was given to me by a friend who wrote on the front inside page of the book:

"I pray that these stories will speak to you—teach you about grace—grace in its most intense form as it occurs in the midst of suffering. I pray that you will find that suspended moment of salvation and hold it—grow in it—transcend it and see God."

That's a more than forty-year-old prayer that a friend prayed and wrote for me and it has stood the test of time.

I don't know how to explain it or articulate it or tell you anything other than it is my expanding path.

Imagine Flannery O'Connor who said that her stories centered on "the offer of grace, usually refused."

Imagine Flannery with a long, nasal southern drawl, who died of lupus at the age of thirty-nine, living on a farm not many miles from where I live today, as she stares into the nothingness of the back of a chifforobe, a musty wooden wardrobe with drawers, and types words of grace into the people she creates, sometimes grotesque characters, and then, of all things, that grace gets into a reader like me.

Ah, the power of the written word, of literature, of poetry and prose. Please read this woman somewhere in your journey.

July 19

Heaven goes by favor. If it went by merit, you
would stay out and your dog would go in.
—Mark Twain

I don't know a lot about heaven or immortality.

I understand those who say, "When you die, you die and that's the end of it," and given the life I have lived, I can say, "All right, I understand. My life has been sweet joy. It has been a great ride. I have walked on Grace Street," but it just seems there does not have to be more, but I believe that there will be more.

I have this sense that whatever heaven is, heaven will be Grace Street into infinity.

It is so much more than a feeble attempt to find a way out of the fear of death. It is the great hope within us. It is not an attempt to justify a bad decision. It is great hope that cannot be explained otherwise.

I was talking about this with Brother Callistus, a monk at the Monastery of the Holy Spirit, the other day, and he lifted his hands into the air and declared with a dance and a loud shout, "It's gonna be a great party!"

July 20

I think there is a letting go on the way to heaven on Grace Street.

Brother Callistus and I had a good talk about it all and he told me about painting *en plein air*. It is a French expression that means "in the open air" or "in the moment," with natural light as the illumination of the subject.

Several prominent artists in the Atlanta area spent a week at the monastery and created some lovely pieces of art. The deeper part of it all has to do with letting go, living in the moment as it exists, and knowing when the painting is finished. This is certainly a monastic virtue as well as a virtue in other forms of spirituality.

It is about detachment. Letting go, surrender, does not always come easily, but perhaps it is the only way to fully live.

We can cling so much to this or that or we can open our hands and let go, engulfed by a grace that never lets go. And what do we have to lose with everything to gain?

July 21

A friend writes during this time of physical need in my own life these words: "In the parlance of our communion (Episcopalian), I wish that your current path may be kept as a holy Lent."

And I think, we've already passed through Lent. Pentecost has come and gone. I am ready to move on. Why another Lent in the midst of a green and growing summer?

But it is as it is and we go on, sometimes in fear and trembling, strength and weakness, fear and hope for the journey is set before us.

When I was in college, I heard the president of the school I attended say something I have never forgotten. It was also forty years ago. The president was quoting some person in history, I do not remember who, and I may not even have his words exactly right, but this is what I remember:

"Pass me through a stern cleansing if I may but serve you, God."

Yes to letting go, surrender, living in the moment, the cleansing in suffering so that we may better learn how to love, how to practice art *en plein air*.

I believe there is, as the old spiritual says, that great gettin' up morning.

The last word of Steve Jobs before he died was "Wow!"

July 22

Richard Rohr writes, "Only the non-dual, contemplative mind can hold both sides of everything, including both death and resurrection . . . Such 'wisdom seeing' allows you to hold the full promise of the Real Life, which is big enough to even include death. Death and life are in an eternal embrace. We cannot have one without the other."

Wendell Berry, my favorite writer, simply says, "Practice resurrection."

I think of the conversations we have had at his farm in Kentucky around the subject. Every day, every single one of us, because of grace and not because of anything we have done or failed to do, has the opportunity to come up out of our graves and practice resurrection in acts of self-denial, of kindness and grace.

July 23

I like what Flannery O'Connor has to say in her short story "A Good Man is Hard to Find" –

"'Jesus was the only One that ever raised the dead.' The Misfit continued, 'And He shouldn't have done it. He thrown everything off balance. If He did what He said, then it's nothing for you to do but throw away everything and follow Him, and if He didn't, then it's nothing for you to do but enjoy the few minutes you got the best way you can.'"

Mattie Powell was a spiritual mentor of mine, perhaps the most influential person in my life other than my mother. Miss Mattie was quite a woman. She lived until she was ninety-six and then she quietly died, but talk about resurrection, talk about a spirit who has lived on, she's one, and there are many people in all our journeys just like Miss Mattie.

For more than thirty years, I would call her up every Easter Day, and she would answer the phone with a resounding, "Christ is risen!"

I would exclaim, "Christ is risen indeed!"

We both would cry out, "Hallelujah!"

I miss her voice immensely, but in her absence, others have picked it up in my personal journey and I know it is the great refrain heard round the world through the ages.

July 24

Who of us does not skip a heartbeat over the joy of Pope Francis, a refreshing spirit, a new voice in an old church?

I like the way he writes of the resurrection in his magnificent book *The Joy of the Gospel*. The pope says that the power and meaning of Jesus's resurrection is not found in the past. He explains the resurrection in terms of a story that calls attention to the persistent power of love and life today:

- Of nature and spring after a long cold winter
- Of goodness in a world that seems governed by evil
- Of light where darkness reigns unabated
- Of justice where injustice is simply taken for granted
- Of beauty where ugliness is worshipped as its opposite
- And of hope over despair

Let us not forget the words of Tony Campolo: "It's Friday, but Sunday's coming."

July 25

I think we get a right good taste of heaven, earth side.

If I could follow any dream, I would take a road trip across the length and breadth of this great land of ours and seek out people along the way just to hear their stories, maybe five a day to give some time to think about what I'd hear.

I would want to look into their eyes, ask them what makes them tick, see them shed a tear or two, and smile at something good. I would seek out drifters searching for a home, diggers in the dirt, farmers, old folks in nursing homes, mamas who work in coffee joints just trying to make a dime, people going through rough times.

I would look for rejects, outcasts, contrarians, rabble-rousers, and discontents. I would search for people who are blowin' smoke, cussin' like a sailor, terribly stirred up.

I would look for local poets who write awful poetry but somehow get a few words down on paper just to try to wake their sleepy souls. I wouldn't mind a talk with a writer who slings out mostly junk but thinks he has it in him to write the greatest story ever told.

I would want to meet birdwatchers and people who give a damn about the earth and know a pretty sunrise when they see one.

If asked, "Hey, man, can you spare me a quarter?" I'd say, "Sure, brother, if you can spare me a story."

I'd ask these people where they hurt—not secondary hurts but the biggest one in the deepest part of their gut. What makes them lonely or sad, laugh or sing? I'd ask them about their regrets and dreams.

July 26

I would get around to a little talk of grace, and some would say, "What's that?"

I would say, "I'm not sure but it's something great inside each of us, something that tells us we are loved just like we are, no strings attached."

And they might say, "You talkin' about God?"

I'd say, "Well, maybe, maybe not. Maybe I'm talking about some moment or person in your life when you felt good or at home with something or someone other than yourself that surprised you out of nowhere."

And then they would tell me a simple story that would blow me away and bring big tears to my eyes, and I'd know I was in the awesome presence of someone just like me who most likely tells quite a different story than mine but that somehow we are caught up in the same love that makes us one family on earth.

I'd say that's grace.

I'd say that's a little bit of heaven.

July 27

The other day an incredible gift came to me. I have never had a poem written for me, but David Garrison, provost and professor of English at LaGrange College, sent me this gift which I will cherish for the rest of my journey.

A Light of Dreams
(for Jeff Blake)

Another summer's on its way. The clock,
Like the heart, repeats itself, indifferent
And blameless. But the heart, always to blame,
Knows only the shape of autumn, only
The long slow going away we all are.
All you living things in the world, know this:
The solstice is as good as it gets, this
One or the other, good as light can be.
But for me, October please, maybe March,
A half-day, half-night world, a light of dreams.
The bluebirds I saw today near the school
Flew across the field without a thought. They
Know love in their cells, their half-lit black eyes
Alert to the way all days roll forward,
The little clocks in their chests clicking on.
Save me something, Saint Patrick, at the end.
Save for me a goat named John, or the pier
That juts into the sea from Tybee, or
A night like this, the summer closing in,
A world in which we fly and fly and fly.

July 28

Wendell Berry in his lovely volume of poetry entitled, *This Day/Collected & New Sabbath Poems,* writes,

Do not live for death,
Pay it no fear or wonder.
This is the firmest law
of the truest faith. Death
is the dew that wets the grass
in the early morning dark.
It is God's entirely. Withdraw
your fatal homage, and live.

When I die, say God's grace was sufficient. Say grace was my constant companion and grace broke the ironclad rules and released me from my self-made prisons. There was no merit badge system.

Say I lived earth-side as fully and joyfully as I could. Say my father, our father, loved me with an unimagined love and would not let me go.

Say it's morning. Say I'm home.

July 29

Pregnant again with the old twins; fear and hope.
-From a eulogy to John Donne

These words from a eulogy to John Donne have captivated my mind and heart for a long time now.

Every word is important—*pregnant*; *again* (not the first time); *with the old* (not the first time); *twins* (twins, maybe joined at the hip and certainly part of the same family); *fear and hope.*

We understand, don't we? We've been there. We live there. Some days we live with fear while on other days we live with hope and then there are those days we live somewhere in the middle. That certainly has been my experience in this journey with cancer.

But I will tell you this. The scales are tipping toward hope in my journey.

The day I had many lymph nodes removed to decrease the possibility of the spread of cancer in my body, my blood pressure was sky-high—at stroke level, I was told—and at the same time, there were moments of centeredness, quiet contemplation, and prayer. I felt the presence of the old twins, fear and hope.

There were all kinds of people around me; some were kind and warm while others were clinical and cold. Some were healers while others were just doing their jobs. I accepted them all as best I could as healing agents in my life.

Someone wrote on the board in the hospital room where I spent the night after surgery, "Hi Jeff! Welcome to your healing habitat!" and so the room became a kind of healing place for the hours I was there. The windows were spacious, and I watched evening come, the night in its serenity, the first light of the morning while listening to quiet streams of music.

July 30

All night, except for perhaps an hour or so, I was awake in a healing habitat of grace.

I was essentially alone though there were a couple of attendants around me through the night. I kept repeating the scripture "Be still and know that I am God," and I was glad for grace as I thought about all the places of healing that occur in my life like grandchildren, books, garden, woods, and music. Hope is a constant in healing habitats.

When the doctor called with the news that all thirty-one of the removed lymph nodes were clear and that there was no cancer, I cried for joy. I was grateful. I was humbled. I was amazed by grace.

Emily Dickinson wrote,

> Hope is the thing with feathers
> That perches in the soul
> And sings the tune without the words
> And never stops at all.

July 31

My journey with cancer has been a story of fear and hope.

Some of what has transpired is like a dream. A heavy shadow is lifting, yet I am still not altogether sure-footed, and at the same time, I am filled with gratitude and I hear those voices that are always calling us to come up out of our graves.

I have tried to articulate what I feel and about the best way I can describe it is to quote some words from Haruki Murakami, a Japanese writer: "And once the storm is over, you won't remember how you made it through, how you managed to survive. You won't even be sure, whether the storm is really over. But one thing is certain, when you come out of the storm, you won't be the same person who walked in. That's what this storm's all about."

I like that. Any long valley, any suffering through which any of us travel, has the potential to be turned into something good and we are never the same again. That is part of what I mean when I write and speak of traveling on Grace Street.

August 1

I have many dreams yet to turn into reality if I am given the gift of time. These dreams are not grandiose; rather they have to do with the nature of learning how to love the earth and all creatures great and small with whom I am one.

The greatest power we are given is the power to love and there is no greater healing power than love. I want to live in solidarity with others, particularly those who suffer through the long night.

I am moved to tears by Mary Oliver's *I Asked Percy How I Should Live My Life*:

Love, love, love, says Percy.
And run as fast as you can
Along the shining beach, or the rubble, or the dust.
Then, go to sleep.
Give up your body heat, your beating heart.
Then, trust.

I believe hope wins through love. I join the voices of people around the world who extol Charles Wesley's hymn *O For a Thousand Tongues to Sing,*

"O for a thousand tongues to sing my great Redeemer's praise, the glories of my God and King, the triumphs of his grace."

Notice, *the triumphs of his grace.* God's grace always triumphs.

August 2

Whatever is happening is the path to enlightenment.
-Pema Chödrön

We will likely go to the Potter's House somewhere along the journey.

Helen Harvey, outside Washington, DC, is a friend of mine and a master potter. She lifted a sentence from something I wrote the other day: "The last time I looked, my feet were made of clay."

She said my words stopped her, and she realized that, in her potting career, *nothing* that did not go through the firing survived. Clay can be melted down, rewedged, and thrown over and over. Until it is fired, it can't speak to others or hold the things that nourish life. Vessels, statues, and all the things on earth made of clay that survive must go through the fire to give them strength and a voice.

She said, "I think you are going through the fire. . . . Your voice will be stronger and even more lasting for whatever more time you have on this earth and, through your written words, beyond."

She finished with "There is a 'cooling down' period when the potter waits to see what miracles have occurred in the kiln, a testimony to faith. We'll all be waiting, knowing that no matter how long your life on this earth, you will leave a permanent legacy."

Yes to the grace of the firing at the Potter's House.

August 3

Wendell Berry says, "To me, at my age, the main question is, 'Can I be a grateful man when I die? Can I remember up to and on the last day that I had a very good life?'"

None of us know the day or the hour of our departure, and most of us have been enjoying the ride more than enough to want to stay earth side as long as we can, assuming we are able to be "value added" (to use a business term) for those around us. All any of us has ever known is to be alive for which we are exceedingly grateful.

A great-grandmother of mine lived from age ninety-four to one hundred and one as a bedridden woman, never apparently knowing though all those years that she was in this world, and I wonder what kind of life would that be.

Life is really exhilarating, but it is also exhausting. A good life is exhausting. It means you have got bumps and bruises and scars, and you've been active and loved much and cried much and laughed a lot.

Ernest Hemingway in *A Farewell to Arms* writes, "The world breaks everyone, and afterwards, many are made strong in the broken places."

And listen to these profound words of Eugene O'Neil: "Man is born broken. He lives by mending. The grace of God is the mending clue."

August 4

Longevity has its place, but the important thing is to live qualitatively as fully as we can whether we sprint or crawl or someone tugs us across the finish line.

Every physician I have these days has been talking to me about mortality. Yes, they talk about life and treatment, but they also are honest enough to tell me, as Paul Harvey used to say, "the rest of the story."

That's where gratitude comes a-knockin'. I have had quite a ride so far, and I would be pleased if it goes on for a good while longer, but the important thing, Berry says, is to be grateful for what has been, what is today, and what may be in the future.

Oh, the kindness of people. People who cross my path make me exceedingly grateful every day. I seem to want to finish off everything I write or say with "I am grateful."

Gratefulness is grace.

August 5

I think of a fellow, a good man in Louisville, who wrote me these humbling and healing words recently:

"Just listening to 'Never Ending Happening' by Bill Fay at home before calling it a night and I was reminded of you and your recent lovely writings, your courage, and your openness to wonder. I just wanted to send this song to you. I listen to it often. . . . It's perhaps the closest reflection of my spirituality I've ever heard in song lyrics . . . and from now on I will think of you along with all the other things that this song calls forth in me. Best wishes, my friend. Thank you for your strength, courage, and eloquence. 'The never ending happening, of what's to be and what has been, just to be a part of it, is astonishing to me' sounds like something you could have written."

August 6

I happened to be at the home of Dr. John Hurd, distinguished and retired professor at LaGrange College in Georgia, on the day he heard his doctor say, "You have three months to live."

He and his lovely wife were among the first people I met when I went to work at the college, and we were friends all the way through until his relatively early death.

I asked John how he intended to live his last days, and I will never forget what he said: "I plan to live my last days just like I have lived my life, as wide open and alive as I can be."

John understood what Emerson meant when he said, "No one suspects the days to be gods."

There was a mighty big funeral at Saint Mark's Episcopal Church in the city of LaGrange to the glory of God and in John's honor when he died.

I never will forget the priest sharing the sacrament of Holy Communion with the congregation and the moment my eyes met the eyes of John's wife as I was returning to my seat. She quietly and beautifully put one thumb up, and I did the same. Thumbs up to a life well lived and to the hope that is within us.

Grace is a thumbs up!

August 7

A wise old priest asked Barbara Brown Taylor, author of *Learning to Walk in the Dark* and so much more, to come speak in his parish. "What do you want me to talk about?" she asked. "Come tell us what is saving your life now," he answered.

That's a pretty good question isn't it? What ultimately matters to you or to me?

I am answering the question every day when it comes to the future of my health. The answer to the question is not the filthy, dirty words I hear all the time in the political world or the pitiful, petty words and the silence I sometimes hear in the religious world.

The people close to me know what the answers are for me. They know the anchors hold. They know I have my moments of anxiousness, but I am in the hands of God, which is a better place to be than any other place I know.

Someone shared with me the other day these magnificent words found in the book *Presage* by Addison Thomas Gutherie:

"There will come a moment in your life when all truth will be known. All the questions, doubts and suspicions you have ever harbored will be instantly answered, but they will no longer be of importance or meaningful. The answers you searched for throughout your life will be insignificant."

What will be significant is that we will have completed our walk on Grace Street earth side and spend eternity in the transition on the same street in whatever lies beyond the veil.

August 8

Frederick Buechner got it exactly right: "Touch, taste, smell, your way to the holy and hidden heart of it because in the last analysis, all moments are key moments and life itself is grace."

He also said, "Here is the world. Beautiful and terrible things will happen. Don't be afraid. I am with you."

Our culture runs from death and will do anything possible to deny the reality of death. We would do well to learn from Buddhist thought that it is very helpful to remind ourselves daily about death and impermanence.

The Dalai Lama says, "Our present lives, however, are not forever. To think 'Death is the enemy' is totally wrong. Death is part of our lives."

August 9

My friend Joanna Adams honored me by writing the foreword for this book. She has spent her vocational life as a Presbyterian minister in large churches in the Atlanta area and in Chicago.

She tells a beautiful story about a father whose heart was broken because his son had run away and gotten into a lot of trouble. The father tried to find him. He pursued him here and there, but it was as if the son had disappeared into another world. Finally, feeling sort of out there himself, the father yelled into empty space, "Son, please come back."

The son heard the father's call. He looked across the great gulf that lay between him and his father. He shouted back, "I can't go that far."

The father said, "Can you meet me halfway?"

The boy said, "No, I can't even do that."

The father answered, "Well, then come as far as you can. I'll come the rest of the way and meet you wherever you are."

Grace meets us wherever we are.

August 10

I remember a beautiful spring afternoon when Stephen, my son, was a little boy. He had been playing all through the day, and when I went out in the late afternoon to bring him home for supper, he looked up at me and said, "Daddy, I've had a busy day. Carry me."

In a much more profound way, that's what our great and faithful God is doing all along the way when we are traveling on Grace Street.

Yes!

. . . For a time
I rest in the grace of the world
and am free.

Wendell Berry

August 11

*Rain is grace; rain is the sky descending to the
earth; without rain, there would be no life.*
-John Updike

In the deepest part of the night, I write the most important
words I choose to share about Grace Street. I write as someone
who embraces Christianity and who respects those who advocate
a different path, for there is no question in my mind that there are
many ways to God.

I gladly sit at a round table with people who are of a different
religion or persuasion than the one I follow, as well as those who
are atheists or agnostics or never spend much time thinking
about the spiritual implications of the journey.

One of the most important things I know about spirituality is
that we are one family and we bring our own cultural identities
and our own histories to the table where we sit together in a
circle of mutuality, and no one is greater or lesser than the other.

That's not just talk or idle words or an attempt to appear open
and receptive to a diversity of thought. It is, in fact, the way it is.

It is as it is.

I write as a seeker, a learner, a discoverer, and someone who
sees through a glass darkly with the hope of seeing more clearly.

What a waste of time it would be, how hypocritical it would
be, to write of traveling on Grace Street if my heart and mind
were not open to differing ways of seeing things or if I thought
for a single moment that my particular view was the only viable
alternative in the vast universe of thought given over to spiritual
matters.

August 12

If it helps to stipulate that many bad things have been done in the history of our world in the name of religion, I confess that the story is replete with excess, abuse, and the perversion that any religion brings to the conversation. Religion has sometimes been more an enemy of God than a friend, and institutions have gotten it wrong over and over again.

There have been centuries stacked upon centuries of ignorance, misguided and flat-out wrong representations of aspects of spirituality. Sadly, we sometimes have survived our man-made institutions while we languished and waited for a clearing, a better day.

When we forget our roots or our original intent, we have every prospect of going off on some deviation of truth or faith or love or grace, but we are not to allow the fringe elements of the great religions of the world to distract us or to keep us from the good, which comes to us by way of true articulation of the basic tenants of religion.

John Philip Newell's recent book, *The Rebirthing of God: Christianity's Struggle for New Beginnings,* is a prophetic word regarding how the world sees Christianity today.

Newell, former leader of Iona Abbey in the Western Isles of Scotland and a wonderful voice in the Celtic expression of Christianity, writes, "The walls of Western Christianity are collapsing. In many parts of the West that collapse can only be described a seismic."

He goes on to offer a way forward, imaging a new birth from deep within Christianity, a fresh stirring of the Spirit.

August 13

But you say, you are not interested in a new birthing of Christianity or any other religion for that matter. And you say, good riddance and finally the world is waking up to what you already knew and that it was all a sham, a fabrication, a hoax, a scheme concocted to put people down instead of building people up, and aren't all religions the same and cutout of the same cloth and isn't "religion the opiate of the people" as Karl Marx hypostasized?

Isn't religion really only a crutch for weak people who are looking for an easy fix, a way out of the hell of their lives, the suffering,the pain, the unknown of the journey?

At the center of it all are the words of C. S. Lewis: "Christianity, if false, is of no importance, and if true, of infinite importance. The only thing it cannot be is moderately important."

It seems to me that Christianity is of infinite importance as are the other great religions of the world. It also seems to me that there will be, somewhere in our frame of reference, someone or something or some other as higher than ourselves, or we will simply choose to be our own gods. We may choose to make ourselves gods and think we are wise enough, smart enough, insightful enough, or intelligent enough to know the ultimate mystery for ourselves, or we may choose to humble ourselves and open our minds and hearts to the possibility that there just may be something more.

August 14

On Grace Street, from my perspective as one who embraces Christianity, there is a cross. Grace streams from that cross and this happens in ways we could never fully understand or articulate.

I am not particularly interested in the various theories as to the meaning of the cross. I certainly do not see the cross in any punitive way; rather I see the cross as the ultimate expression of love for the whole world.

It is a love I cannot fully articulate. It is greater than my ability to comprehend. Call me old-fashioned, out of date, unaware, or whatever you may choose. I prefer to "cling to the old rugged cross" and not to my intellect or my speculations or to any of the theories as to what happened on the cross.

Something great happened on the cross, something amazing, something of mystery that changed the course of human history.

And it wasn't just those who choose to believe who were affected. The whole creation was affected. The entire human family was affected in ways we cannot grasp.

That's part of why I accept the universality of grace for all people whether they choose to believe or not, and that is why traveling on Grace Street is so important to me and so central to my journey.

The cross is the yes of God for all people. As Desmund Tutu says, "All means all."

August 15

The great symbol of God for me is the one of God as the Suffering Servant.

We may talk of the God of tenderness who said, "Let the little children come unto me," or the God who is the Good Shepherd or the Teacher who gave us the beatitudes or the One who gently knocks at the door, but the great image of God for me is the one where God lies as a baby in a lowly manger, makes of himself no reputation, takes upon himself the form of a servant, gets down on his knees with a towel and a basin, and washes his disciples' feet as the whole world hears the gentle splashing of water in a basin.

The great image of God is the one where God bears a cross on the way to a hill where love wins and where ultimately resurrection occurs in the middle of the darkest night.

My home is full of art and the great symbols I have gathered through the years of my journey. I am surrounded by beauty and signs that call me to think higher, lovelier, loftier thoughts.

There are many renderings of the prodigal son and the loving father in my home.

There are crosses from many places in the world where I have traveled, but the one symbol that I treasure most is the one my mother brought me back from Rome, proudly telling me that it had been blessed by the pope.

It is a crucifix of Jesus, of the Suffering Servant, pouring out nothing but love for the whole human race.

That's the ultimate expression of Grace Street as far as I am concerned.

It is my hope, my anchor, my life, my salvation, my deliverance, my love, the place from which grace streams to a needy world of people who are hungry, not for judgment but for unconditional, no-strings-attached love.

August 16

There are some things I would be willing to maybe
even bet my life on . . . that life is grace.
-Frederick Buechner

The homestretch has every possibility of carrying us all the way to the house on Grace Street.

The length of this stretch of the journey is unknown, thus its power to shape us in the image of love where we live on the palatable cutting edge of life. This grace becomes a never-ending discovery in waiting, trusting, and living in the moment.

Grace is an anchor in a weary land and has certainties and also unknown entities. It is therefore best surrendered and lived out in the Hands of God.

We need not fear grace because love casts out fear and leaves us in a place of presence. Fear is our human dimension, but love is our abiding place, our eternal home.

We were born in original love, not sin, and we will die in this same love.

August 17

Let us not tell ourselves that we are anything but love or less than enough. It is the chattering mind which distracts us from the love we always have been and always will be. We must not allow our minds to control our hearts. We live out of our hearts.

Pema Chödrön said, "We're actually complete and whole. There is nothing wrong fundamentally with us." How could there be, since we were made in the Image of Love?

There is no condemnation in grace. We sometimes condemn ourselves or allow other people to condemn us, but grace does not condemn.

Frederick Buechner writes of the shimmering self, and so in fact, we are all beautiful and made to shine like the sun, as observed of busy people at the corner of Fourth and Main in Louisville, Kentucky by Thomas Merton.

August 18

The great reality is the moment, or "the Naked Now," as Richard Rohr would say.

The Now is the only place where we can fully live. It's the place where we breathe in and breathe out. Yesterday is gone and tomorrow may never come, but we have this moment today.

We are invited to speak whatever our truth is in our own voices, in our own unique ways. We share our lives in vulnerability, fragility, and openness. It's the only way to live.

Our voices may be weak and fragile, but our hearts are strong in the power of grace.

August 19

Whatever awareness we will have at the moment of death is a mystery.

Who can fathom the deep, deep love of God? Who can measure the immeasurable grace we have been given? Who knows what tomorrow may bring?

Fracture, loss, sickness, or pain? Yes, possibly, for such is the nature of the journey, but there is more, and there is abundantly more. We are in all things more than conquerors

Grace is like a thread running through our lives that is more than adequate for every circumstance, every detour, and every step we take, and nothing can separate us from this grace.

It is never about me. It is never about you. It is always about tapping into the amazing grace of Love.

August 20

Our vision is sometimes blurred or impaired, which means we must clean our lens and begin to see clearly. Not as clearly as we will see, but our world changes as we set our feet on a path of grace with a clean lens.

Once we get into the flow of grace and have our lens cleaned, we begin to realize we were love from the beginning and will still be love in the end.

The years take on magnificent meaning.

Grace carries us all the way home, especially when we are right in the middle of our worst moments. Let us not stop or give up. We'll be home after a little while.

Someone said, "I do not understand the mystery of grace, only that it meets us where we are and does not leave us where it finds us." Who could plumb the depths of the mystery of grace?

August 21

A skeptical fellow traveler from halfway around the world wrote me, "Grace may very well be the doorway."

I say grace is the doorway to the experience of beauty where all the messiness of the journey mingles and becomes one with the greater. It is in this house on Grace Street where gratitude comes out the doors and windows like music.

Grace is the doorway of the home where all are invited to the party and sit at a roundtable to enjoy the Feast.

Kathleen Norris wrote, "If grace is so wonderful, why do we have such difficulty recognizing and accepting it? Maybe it's because grace is not gentle or made-to-order. It often comes disguised as loss, or failure, or unwelcome change."

August 22

Richard Rohr helps answer the question Kathleen Norris poses: "The flow of grace through us is largely blocked when we are living inside a worldview of scarcity, a feeling that there's just not enough: enough of God, enough of me, enough food, enough mercy to include and forgive all faults."

A churchman recently scoffed at my perspective on grace. Surprisingly, he thinks we must live in a house of shame, guilt, and fear. He is my neighbor, but I choose to live in a house of grace.

How could anyone choose to live in a house of fear? But we do, don't we?

Isn't it a fact we sometimes register our opposition to God's grace?

"That's an easy, mushy anything-goes, pie-in-the-sky, sweet-by-and-by way of living," he pushed back.

"Au contraire," I suggested. "Opening up to grace and living grace with others is far more challenging than anything I know.

August 23

There's no cheap grace.

Grace costs everything.

It is Richard Rohr who said, "Grace is the divine Unmerited Generosity that is everywhere available, totally given, usually undetected as such, and often even undesired."

I have been considering, even testing grace for many years.

Grace is the one great thought and experience that captivates me.

That's why I wrote *Living on Grace Street* and *More Travels on Grace Street* and *Homestretch, This Journey of Grace Street*.

These memoirs become a kind of reality check and I am sharing my voyage as honestly as I am able.

We all have stories to tell – stories of grace.

August 24

The most transformative time in my journey on Grace Street has come later in life, in what I am calling "the Homestretch."

Hear the majestic words of Ramakrishna, "The winds of God's grace are always blowing. It is for us to raise our sails."

I am as *Come Thy Fount,* the old hymn, suggests, "Oh to grace, how great a debtor."

August 25

"You were born with wings, why prefer
to crawl through life?"
—Rumi

All of us are on a grace journey—journeys that are uniquely different yet carry some of the same longings and aspirations, the same struggle and joy.

I think we were born to walk together, to take each other's hands, to consider deeply our oneness in the human family. We do not live well in isolation for we are part of each other. We are inescapably bound to each other, which is why we must build bridges, not walls of separation.

Solitude is one thing. Community is another. They are hand in glove and are essential to a good journey. The simple truth is, we need each other.

August 26

I need you to hold me to the Light as I hold you to the Light.

Traveling becomes not a burden, but a delight when we make the journey together.

The journey is no greater distance than to our hearts. We may travel the world, but it is the distance to our hearts that makes all the difference.

The awakening of the heart is where we find light and life and love, not darkness, not sin, but Love at the core of our being, which transforms us and the world around us.

August 27

The grace journey is not about building walls. It is about building bridges. Grace is not about crawling. Grace is about flying.

A young friend sent me an 11-word text that rattled my world: *Go outside. Find a star and I will meet you there.*

As an aging man in a cynical and skeptical world, I am still dreaming.

I am still hoping. I still believe that every day is the best day of the journey and, regardless of what comes, that Love is the core.

Love is the house on Grace Street.

By the way, traveling on Grace Street will carry us all the way to the house. We may get lost on the way, but we will get home.

August 28

Lyndon Marcotte, a fellow-traveler in Louisiana, told me the story of his grandfather's death.

Lyndon's grandfather was his first hero, the man who was right by his side in his earliest adventures.

Lyndon was by his grandfather's side in the final moments of his life earth-side.

Lyndon said his hand was on his grandfather's heart while the family gathered around singing "Amazing Grace."

He said he knew his grandfather died at about verse three of the six verses, but so as not to disturb his grandfather's transition into deeper grace or not further unsettle the family members, he continued to lead them in singing.

Grace means we keep singing.

August 29

For Kathleen Singh, a friend in Florida who is a caregiver and writer and has been with hundreds of people when they died, the moment of death is was always beautiful.

Recently our beloved Kathleen made the transition herself.

The process of getting there may be excruciatingly painful, but the moment of release and surrender, when we exhale our last breath, is beautiful.

The Apostle Paul said two thousand years ago wrote, "Whether we live or die, we belong to God."

I take that to mean that from our birth to our death and beyond, we belong to Love. Yes, we belong to grace.

Ram Dass says, "We're all just walking each other home."

I know this: "Life's a journey." Life's a journey, a long path, divergent paths, multiple paths, mountains and valleys, joys and sorrows, darkness and light, sunsets and sunrises, gains and losses, failures and victories, with some mighty great walking step by step into the Naked Now.

This moment, this is the moment we have been given.

Richard Rohr thunders the truth, "Death is not a changing of worlds as most imagine, as much as the walls of this world infinitely expanding."

August 30

Every great Grief conceals a great Grace.
God does for us what we would do for our own children.
The trials and pains of 'growing up' bring us closer to Him.
-A Carthusian, *They Speak by Silences*

We will not be very far along our travels on Grace Street when the fractures will likely come.

The fractures often shake us to our core and leave us vulnerable and uncertain. They are often for our ultimate well-being, but we do not always recognize them as such. They come as aliens, strangers, and enemies. When they come, as they surely will, what are we to do?

Our natural instinct is to run and not hold steady in the water. Fractures hurt and create pain. How could they possibly be grace?

Except they are. Believe it or not, they are.

August 31

When I wrote *Traveling on Grace Street*, a fellow-traveler protested, "You make everything grace."

She did not realize it, but she had critiqued the writing exactly as I intended.

Richard Rohr and many other spiritual writers are direct and to the point: Everything is grace.

A fracture may be anything that causes us discomfort or to be troubled.

Fractures expose our nakedness and fragility, something common to the whole human family.

Eckhart Tolle says, "For most people, their spiritual teacher is their suffering. Because eventually the suffering brings about awakening."

A fracture may be an illness, the death of a loved one, a divorce, a child in rebellion, the loss of a job, a financial crisis, or doubt as to the certainty of what you have been taught to believe all your life about God. You name it.

Life is difficult, and even when it is not, we make it so.

I was standing at the grave of Thomas Merton at the Abbey of Gethsemani in Kentucky when my cell phone rang. I knew it was my doctor in Atlanta. He was calling to tell me another melanoma outside my rib cage had been confirmed. That was a moment of fracture where grace took over.

September 1

We are told by Frederick Buechner: "The world is beautiful. The world is terrifying." And so it is.

The world is broken and we are broken or fractured and could use some grace surgery. Grace Street travelers are healers, treating ourselves and others with the medicine of grace.

We could easily live by our illusions. You know, ones like invincibility, strength, power, even the foolishness that we will live forever.

We could live by the illusion that a bigger house, a substantial portfolio, an impressive resume, a collection of acquaintances, a certain set of beliefs, and all the rest is where it's at; but then the fractures come and we are shaken as layers and layers of the false self are stripped away.

September 2

And what will we find when we get to the core of it all? Not that we are ugly or evil. At the core of our being, we will find that we are Love. We always were. We always will be, which means the fractures become grace.

This Love, this grace, becomes the source of the healing of our wounds.

I will never forget that day in Lexington, Kentucky, when a small group of us were exploring Frederick Buechner's book, *Telling Secrets*. We were an elite little group, awfully satisfied with our spirituality. I don't know how she ever got into our circle, but she did. She told us she was a woman off the street the street where she had been selling her body to feed the lust of the flesh of men who bought her for a few dollars.

I imagine that woman had known more than her share of fractures.

We were talking about Buechner's idea that all people are love at the core of their being. You see, it's not such a foreign thought after all, though in our self-righteousness we attempt to somehow earn what is already our inheritance.

September 3

We fight grace; we fight love, tooth and toenail.

The woman off the street stopped us dead in our tracks, and there was silence. She questioned, "You mean I am a beautiful woman and that if somehow the layers and layers of me were peeled away, I would find at the core of who I am that I am love?"

"Yes!" we said. There was a chorus of agreement. And in that quiet place of utter fracture, I began to discover that what others had told me negatively about myself was not at all true.

Grace began to stir in me.

Perhaps it was the place where I first took a tiny step onto Grace Street, that step that has made all the difference in the world.

September 4

Hardly a week passes that someone does not tell me about a fracture in their lives. I invariably tell them to be encouraged because your fracture is where grace gets in, or as Leonard Cohen would say, our broken cracks are where the light gets in.

Fractures, yes of course, but grace is greater than the sum total of all our fractures.

My journey as a gay man has been meaningful in so many ways. I have learned not to live in the shadows after many years of struggle. I have learned and experienced the truth that I have always been love.

Coming out is a long journey, and we all must take whatever time we need to put the pieces of the puzzle together, and when we do, what a picture it is.

By grace, I am glad to say that I will die someday with nothing hidden and everything I know in the light.

Cathy Edgett, beloved friend in California, gently pushed me over the cliff and helped me to land smack-dab in the middle of the love I always was and will be.

September 5

A young gay man sent me a text which brought tears to my eyes. He wrote, "I often have trouble with my sexuality, but because it has brought me to someone so kind, thoughtful, and wise as you makes me thankful I am the way I am. Your view on life is what I model mine after."

Henri Nouwen said it best when he said we are wounded healers. In a world of fractures, we are grace to each other. And it is in our grace wounds that we are most effective as healers for each other.

One of my most treasured books is *The Divine Yes* by E. Stanley Jones.

I return to the book over and over again. Jones suffered a paralyzing stroke, a near-fatal fracture when he was in his late eighties.

Here's what he decided to do about it. He said Yes to what life handed him, and he recalled, "At last the Divine Yes has sounded." In a naysaying world, we keep saying Yes to life regardless.

Life hands us a "No," and we say "Yes!"

September 6

I have always loved the imagery of the Potter's House. It is the imagery I return to over and over again because it is the nature of love. It may well be a place of fracture and you will always find this house on Grace Street.

You've been there? Of course you have. Contrary to popular opinion, it's a pretty wonderful place.

The Potter's House is that place where the clay is shaped and formed by the hands of the potter whose loving intent is to take the plain-though beautiful clay as it already is and create something even more beautiful.

The molding is really a good thing because the clay and the potter are somehow saying a profound yes to each other. The clay may wonder what's happening, but the clay is in the hands of love, where the heart is.

September 7

We all know something about fear, don't we?

Fear is the predominant thing robbing us of the ability to know in the inner recesses of our hearts that we are love, and that fear keeps us from loving others. Fear divides us, keeps us from one another. Fear causes us to build walls and not bridges.

Fear is a thief in the night robbing us of sleep. It haunts us down and keeps us from love. Fear and love are chief ompetitors in the journey.

• A man loses his male partner after fifteen years of life together and wonders how he will ever make it through the holidays.
• A friend of many years worries that the mass in her lungs may be cancer.
• A young friend in his twenties struggles with his sexuality, refusing to believe he really is OK just like he is.

Fear can make us think and say some awful things about ourselves but our chattering minds are not who we are. We are made for presence, the presence of love which has been the nature of our hearts from the very beginning.

September 8

Recently a woman in Seattle wrote and said she was "a stinker."

Her self-description prompted me to write about how you couldn't prove it by me because I see her in a very different light. For years, I have known her to be an extraordinary woman of love.

I wrote her back, "There are boatloads of self-described stinkers trying desperately to make it to shore. They were sold a bill of goods about unworthiness and so much more that has sometimes distorted their view of who they really are. They are beautiful. They are love. At the core of our being, we are and have always been Love."

September 9

A woman on an island off the coast of Maryland picked up the conversation: "'Mercy,' 'grace,' 'Tao,' 'that which has no name.' Maybe just love? And the greatest of these is charity, a.k.a. love. And thus is my theology on this bright and sunny morning with Christmas music coming from the radio."

Can you hear Ms. Emily Dickinson speaking? "Hope is the thing with feathers that perches in the soul."

Can you take to heart what L. R. Knost said? "Life is amazing. And then it's awful. And then it's amazing again. And in between the amazing and awful it's ordinary and mundane and routine. Breathe in the amazing, hold on through the awful, and relax and exhale during the ordinary. That's just living heartbreaking, soul-healing, amazing, awful, ordinary life. And it's breathtakingly beautiful."

September 10

The writer who sang of the birth of Jesus affirms, "The hopes and fears of all the years are met in thee tonight."

I have been striking up conversations with people on the subject of fear and hope for a very long time.

I wonder what your story of fear and hope is?

Let's have a conversation.

I invite us to sit together and have a chat.

What if we just lay way back in the Presence of the love already in us?

What if we just put our anchors down in this love? What if we just laugh out loud with abandoned hilarity in the grace we all have been given?

A little laughter will chase the blues away. A good laugh, regardless of circumstances, may be the best medicine we can take. Swallow it with compassion and kindness and the grace which carries us all the way home.

September 11

The mystic Hafiz said, "Ever since happiness heard your name, it has been running through the streets trying to find you." Let us be found by grace – the amazing grace of God.

September 12

The thinking mind cannot understand presence.
—Eckhart Tolle

He graciously asked, "Do you wake in person or Presence?"

The way we live out the answer to this question is at the core of core of traveling on Grace Street.

I will honestly tell you from the outset that I have mostly awakened in person, and in fact, most of my days have been lived out in person. It is this journey in Presence to which I am sensing a greater call.

Life and aging have a natural way of calling us to the *being* part of the journey, while in our younger days, we were full of *doing*. A brush with mortality is a grace moment because it forces you to consider more carefully what it means to *be*.

September 13

While in our former days, we are given over to doing, our latter days lend themselves to being. I think that's what Richard Rohr is getting at in *Falling Upward,* his marvelous book on the two halves of life.

In the first half of life, we build the house where we will live and we are mostly ego driven. In the second half of life, we begin to live in the house we have built and to more fully experience what it means to live or to be.

Rohr and others, including Thomas Merton, call this the journey from the False Self to the True Self.

Does it always work out like this? Well, of course not. I have known some beautiful people in the first half of their lives who are beginning to walk in immense authenticity, and I have also known some beautiful people in the second half of their lives who have not a clue, as they are as ego driven as ever.

Perhaps it depends in part on how many wounds we acquire over the years or how often life chisels away at our being and begins to make of us something even lovelier.

September 14

It is not about ritual, or doctrine, or dogma, or teachings, or institutions that sometimes lead only to the chattering mind. It is about the heart. It is about glory. It is about Presence.

The other day, I woke in person. It was not a pretty sight. Usually after a night of sleep, I wake up refreshed and renewed, ready to live the day. But not the morning to which I refer. I was anxious, troubled, fearful, disquieted within.

The chattering mind was racing along, and I wasn't sure

I was living on Grace Street. The mind will sometimes tell me that I don't know much about grace and certainly do not live grace. But that's the pesky mind, not my heart.

The chattering mind will do a number on us. It will have us thinking we are not good enough, not able to face what life flings in our direction, but that's the chattering mind and not our hearts, where Presence resides.

September 15

I like the conversation Anne Lamott had with Wendell Berry on a cold, dark mid-December day at a Book Depot in Mill Valley, California.

Berry says quietly, "It gets darker and darker and darker, and then Jesus is born."

Lamott says, "I love that so much."

I keep saying this, and I repeat: We are called to live in our hearts and not in our minds. We may trust our hearts, for they are made of Presence; they are Love, pure Love.

September 16

I love the mornings. I like to wake while it is still night and the whole world is still and quiet.

The morning glory is most often everywhere outside my window and in my room, where I meditate.

I love the moments when morning breaks against the eastern sky and my chattering mind has not had time to think very much at all. It's what E.Stanley Jones, the missionary to India, called his "Listening Post."

There is enough noise to choke a horse as the day goes on, so I run to the woods, or take a walk, or consider the birds of the air, or read a book, or have a conversation with a fellow traveler, or try to lend a helping hand.

September 17

The most important thing I do is pray, or, as millennials and people in other stages of the journey like to say and practice, I meditate. Meditation is a growing way of living in the world of spirituality.

But you say you have no time to meditate. If you have time to breathe—and you do or you will die—you have time to meditate.

Just to breathe in and out, to still the chattering mind, to focus on something beautiful. Just shutting my mouth and being quiet helps me get into Presence.

Breathe in hope. Breathe in peace. Breathe in quietness. Breathe in love, the Love already within. Breathe out fear. Breathe out anxiety. Breathe out worry. Breathe out noise. This mindful, intentional breathing ritual moves me from restlessness to restfulness, to solitude of the heart. This is Presence.

September 18

I remember a time of meditation with Greg Kirby. There was no struggle, just the Yes, like a flower opening to the sun. When we came to the end of a more deliberate time of meditation, breathing in and out,

Greg asked me how it all went. I could only whisper, "The Presence, only the Presence."

Grace is the presence, only the presence.

September 19

There is that verse in the first chapter of the book of John where there is a reference to "Grace upon grace." William Barclay said the idea of the writer in the verse is like standing on the shore of the great ocean, with wave after wave splashing onto your feet, and he translates the verse as "Wave after wave of grace."

September 20

A righteous man dies and comes before Father Abraham. "I have obeyed the law," says the man. "I've been generous, nurtured my family, taken care of the widow and orphan. I've studied. I've served my community."

"Ah." Father Abraham nodded. "But did you dance?"
I think we may dance well when we are in Presence, or at least tap our toes and snap our fingers.

Some unknown soul says, "When you realize how perfect everything is, you will tilt your head back and laugh at the sky." Richard Rohr says, "We're already in the Presence. What's missing is awareness."

I whisper, "The Presence. Only the Presence."

September 21

And so you have a life that you are living only now,
now and now and now, gone before you can speak of it,
and you must be thankful for living day by day,
moment by moment . . .
a life in the breath and pulse and living light of the present . . .
—Wendell Berry, *Hannah Coulter: A Novel*

It's true, isn't it?

Yesterday's gone and tomorrow may never come, but we have this moment today.

All of our past, regardless of the content, is past. Our future? Unknown but to God alone.

Two of the most influential books in my life have been Eckhart Tolle's *The Present Now* and Richard Rohr's *The Naked Now*. These writings are at once liberating and freeing from the chains of the past and a radical call to live in the present.

We bog ourselves down in senseless regret, mulling over the past; our mistakes, failures, and not-yet places. We do ourselves in if we do not keep the past in perspective. The measurement is never perfection. The measurement is grace. In our imperfections, there is grace, or else it would not be grace.

September 22

Every single one of us is perfectly imperfect. We are not defined by our very worst moment.

I know how to pull out an old memory and embellish it. I know how to put old things in a shadow box, wrap old things in a rubber band, pack old things away for another day. An old saint, an old love, an old idea, a moment can become someone or something that never was, except in my illusions.

I've heard it said that life is just a dream anyway.

I know how to think "futuristic" about what might be, could be, and should (a word I would just as soon regurgitate) be but never turns out as an actuality.

September 23

My chattering mind becomes an acrobat of this and that. Do I live in the past, not the "good," as opposed to the "bad," or as it really was or is?

Do I fly away into the future high and free or keep it safe and close to the ground?

Do I live in spheres which never were, or could be, or will really never be?

Do I allow my wild imagination to take me to a way-off future place that will never be?

And then I sense something greater saying, "Stop. Stop. Stop. Just stop."

My life is not my past or my future. My life is now. This very moment.

September 24

Grace is mostly downstream, but culture and, surprisingly, sometimes the religious world is often upstream.

We can easily complicate it all with our dogma and doctrine, our ritualistic tribalism, and our insistence on doing almost to the exclusion of being. All our learning amounts to too little, all our self-help books will not amount to much, until we get into the flow of the Now.

The Now is where the light is. Don't wait till tomorrow to reach out with loving arms of compassion. Don't wait till later to say, "I love you. I care. I am grateful. You are beautiful." I like the way Walt Whitman puts it: "Pointing to another world will never stop vice among us; shedding light over this world can alone help us."

And you say, "Tomorrow I will do such and such." And I say that there may not be a tomorrow. Seize the day. Cherish the hour. Embrace the moment.

September 25

Live every day like you are dying, not in some morbid, neurotic, or narcissistic way, but in the hope and joy of this very moment.

God is in me as me now, not when I have it all figured out or have all the answers because that day will never come, and so we learn to live with the questions.

Thomas Merton says, "What we have to be is who we are."

The blessed truth is, we are fully known, fully loved *NOW*.

No need to clean up or tidy up or dress up because it's a come-as-you-are party. Why not just wake up and get your dancing shoes on?

September 26

In this now, listen to the words of Hafiz:

When all your desires are distilled;
You will cast just two votes;
To love more
And be happy.

September 27

Richard Rohr comes along and says, "Both God's truest identity and our own True Self are Love," and he challenges us to "live and fully accept our *present* reality."

Rohr writes, "We do not find our own center; it finds us. Our own mind will not be able to figure it out. We collapse back into the Truth only when we are spiritually naked and free, which is probably not very often."

A new perspective is beginning to dawn on me. We are not our dogma, doctrine, or denomination.

September 28

We are not our nationality, race, religion, or creed. We are not our politics, heritage, or culture. We are not our flags, neither Confederate nor American nor Rainbow. We are not Christian or Jew or Muslim. We are not male or female. We are not our sexuality. We are not our work or retirement, nor our health or sickness or money or lack of money. Some of those are often ego designations and not our true selves.

We are not our past or our future. We are now love and share one common humanity, our oneness interwoven in the spirituality of love. This means we do not judge others, for we are essentially and fundamentally love. We are not smart enough, wise enough, insightful enough, and certainly not God enough to judge others.

September 29

Let us celebrate the love we see now in the mirror. Let us embrace the love found in every woman and man.

Love is the essence of who we are, and when we come to this discovery, the whole world changes. Oh how we count and measure and weigh.

How easy to miss the meaning of mercy and to never figure out what grace is all about. The ego is hell-bent on thinking we earn something.

There must be something we do to court the mercy and favor and grace of God. I say we need a conversion, a new way of living where we throw the ledger book out the window and see everything as grace.

September 30

Anne Lamott declares, "We catch grace like we are filling a tin cup at a waterfall."

Richard Rohr keeps saying, "Basically, grace is God's first name, and probably last too."

I believe. I declare. I desire to live in this first and last name for God.

Now and now and now.

To see a World in a Grain of Sand
And a Heaven in a Wild Flower,
Hold Infinity in the palm of your hand
And Eternity in an hour.

William Blake from Augries of Innocence

I am still learning.

Michelangelo, age 88

October 1

Everyone wants to understand art. Why not try to
understand the songs of a bird?
-Picasso, 1923

Nature is the church I love most.

Simply put, the first act of Divine Creation was nature. The first Bible was nature.

Call me what you will. Labels are increasingly unnecessary for my survival. But if you must conjure up a way to describe me, say I walk alongside people like Emerson and Thoreau and in our day, people like John Philip Newell, who somehow experience transcending grace in nature.

Newell, a leader in Celtic spirituality, says, "In every religion we find the need to consecrate our participation in the natural world. This is especially evident in the tribal religions of native peoples. Their songs and prayers express a great courtesy toward the natural world."

I bow in the natural world. I fall to my knees in the dirt of the earth because I believe that to go deep into the Presence of grace in the soil is to experience the Creator who holds all things together as One.

October 2

Nature is grace because it is a pathway out of our chattering minds. How easily we get lost in thinking and fretting and worrying with our chattering minds. The morning headlines are simply overwhelming and more than we can bear. There is enough of any one problem to drive us to distraction.

Nature reminds us of what we forget. Nature calls us to be still and to be ourselves and to live in the Presence of the moment.

Saint Columbanus (543-21 November 615) said, "Understand the creation if you would wish to know the Creator. For those who wish to know the great deep must first review the natural world."

October 3

Nature emanates from the heart, the place where we are who we are.

That's why we are home there and understand our Oneness with all creation.

We live in a noisy world on a merry-go-round.

We are inundated by noise primarily in our own chattering minds.

We are bombarded by noise on the cable news networks, our indispensable gadgets and gizmos, which take us away from relationships and community, and even our work and extracurricular activity.

October 4

This is an underlying theme in the writings of Wendell Berry as he laments what has happened to us in an age when industrialization rules and the machine is a god we have created for our worship.

This is part of what Richard Louv, author of *Last Child in the Woods,* is talking about when he says our children are disconnected from the out-of-doors and tied to things.

We are beyond exhaustion by the time the sun goes down, and then we start all over again once the sun comes up in the morning. It's an unsettling cycle, isn't it?

We are sometimes as addicted to noise as we are to our prescription drugs that are intended to calm us down.

It's pretty much everywhere; this unrelenting noise that destroys equilibrium and causes us to think we are up to something good, when in fact our health and well-being may be damaged.

October 4

Noise is a plague on our spiritual paths. Our religious institutions propagate busyness as a sign of spirituality, when in fact all our running around is sometimes a sign of our final gasping, dying institutional breath.

To borrow the title of an old book, there is the noise of solemn assemblies. Strutting around under the false illusion that we are up to something good when we may be trying to fill the empty holes within and to make ourselves look "hip" and "hot" and "with it" to ourselves and others.

This happens when we are more prone to doing than to being, more engaged with our minds than with our hearts. Religion is about the heart, mind, and body, but at the core of it is the heart which must be still and nourished to grow.

Deep and meaningful prayer goes out the window when we think we can run our religious institutions just as easily by ourselves with our own ingenuity and creativity as we can by leaning into the Source.

All of this has been the story of a major part of my journey. I am drawn like a deer to streams of living water when it comes to stillness.

This thirst for quiet and solitude is partly fulfilled in nature, the original temple. When we return over and over again to the earth, to the ground of being in the dirt, we are beginning to understand what the Psalmist meant when he talked about being like a tree planted by the rivers of living water.

October 5

The call of Celtic spirituality and the eastern religions to listen, to wait, to pay attention is part of my refuge. People will fill the void with mystery and something more if the old cisterns go dry.

My hunger is fulfilled in seasons at the monastery where the monks chant the psalms. My desire is satisfied in a good book, which helps me to center and gain perspective when I could so easily lose my way. This longing for something more than noise is answered in meditation at a listening post and in the multiple ways at my fingertips to pray.

Every time I am in that confining and constricting machine, that cylinder for a scan, I remember the words, "Be still and know that I am God."

Jesus gives an imperative. He speaks not as a suggestion, but in the imperative tense when he says, "Consider (literally 'look at') the birds of the air; they do not sow or reap or store away in barns, and yet your heavenly Father feeds them."

Let me spend my time with the birds in nature.

October 6

There isn't time—so brief is life—for bickering,
apologies, heart-burnings, callings to account. There is only
time for loving—and but an instant, so to speak, for that.
-Mark Twain

Oh the journey, the blessed journey on Grace Street with fellow travelers.

How immeasurably rich is this life we have been given to walk alongside each other. There is no one running ahead and no one lagging behind. If we feel faint or fall, another traveler helps us get up and keep going. We are together, bound inexorably to each other. We are good company. We are as unique and as different as daylight and dark, and this is where we find our strength to be the beautiful tapestry we are.

The underside of the tapestry looks like a jumble of threads, but when the work of art is complete and we turn it over, we see something absolutely beautiful and perfect.

October 7

What seems like falling apart could actually be falling together.

We are to each other salt and light and anchors in the land of the living and the dead.

We were uniquely made for each other to live in grace so freely given to each and every one of us.

Build a wall between us, and it will come tumbling down.

Build a bridge, a multiplicity of bridges, and we will find our paths to Grace Street, where we live as neighbors for each other.

October 8

Friends, whom I often call fellow travelers, are splendid,
radiant lights in their shimmering selves of love. It is said that a
man is rich if he has a handful of friends. I am blessed with
several handfuls of people who are my mentors in grace. I see
your faces. I know your names. I know your names: faith, hope,
and love.

It would take more than a book—in fact it would take several
books—to tell you about all these people and the stories of the
fellow travelers with whom I have intersected. I have written
about a few of them in *Traveling on Grace Street, More Travels
on Grace Street,* and *Homestretch, This Journey on Grace Street.*

October 9

Greg Kirby poured out grace into my life and tirelessly and consistently gave of himself to enhance the love already in my heart.

I remember the first time I met him over lunch in Atlanta. I sensed at the table as we broke bread that I was in the presence of Love.

The human vessel was sitting across from me, but there was something more than a vessel. There was Presence. There was an inseparable bond of friendship from the moment I laid eyes on this man.

Fellow-travelers come and go and very often this is true in the providence of God. Grace profoundly occurs when friends stay.

October 10

I hope you have friends like Greg Kirby. I am sure you do. You see their faces. You know their names. You know how different your life is because they walked into your house on Grace Street one day and began to turn your world upside down.

.   Here are some notes I jotted down about what I have learned from Greg. Just a little of a whole lot I have learned while walking alongside Greg on Grace Street:

• It is this oneness with the whole human family on earth, as well as all creatures great and small, which transforms life.

• All sit at one round table where Divine Love is the feast. Divine Love does not separate us from each other. In fact, this Love brings us intimately together as one family, and it was always true from our beginnings.

• During these hours, my friend and I have kind of drifted, or perhaps providentially entered into, a conversation on the chattering mind, the chattering ego, which is a prison of our making, and we have focused on an alternative which is quietness, solitude, or the recognition of the Presence, the yes of unconditional love.

• This love is not a doing, but a being.

• I am not my thoughts. I am not even my actions. I am Presence. I am love, and so are we all. Contrary to outward appearances, sometimes to the ego-driven eye, we are all beautiful.

• We are not walking away from ourselves; rather, we are walking as ourselves, which means we are perfect. But don't let the word "perfect" trip you up, for this perfection is oneness. The oneness I have begun to articulate in a few words above.

October 11

• Mindfulness, meditation, contentedness, or prayer are at the core of Presence and is a way we break out of our prisons and become free. Here is the Light, the hope within us. Already within us. Always.

• Here is the place we move from our delusional existence which is fear and always a sense of lacking, into abundance, the reality, or as some call it, the true self. The false self is ego based and tells us that we are not Divine Love and that we are terribly lacking, when in fact nothing could be further from the truth.

• Fractures, or the breaking open of our lives, are generally the way we come to the center, to the core of our being where Love has always and will always be. Fractures, which are often painful, are how the light gets in. We say yes to our fractures.

**Be like the sunflower –
Turn away from the darkness
and follow the light.**

-Unknown

October 12

"Laughter is the closest thing to the grace of God."
-Karl Barth

Right in the middle of all this serious reflection (that's funny), I wanted to write a word about laughter.

The words of Karl Barth seem entirely appropriate. Barth was a German thinker who is sometimes referred to as the greatest Protestant theologian of the twentieth century. He had a great understanding of the correlation between grace and laughter.

I have never forgotten one of the best stories out of his journey on the serious matter of love.

He was asked to name his most profound thought. He responded, "The most profound thought I ever had was, 'Jesus loves me this I know for the Bible tells me so.'"

In his brilliance, I imagine he knew something about the simple, spontaneous eruption of pure joy that comes from somewhere deep inside us.

October 13

We're pretty wound up and strung out sometimes. I know I can be, but it is in those moments of letting go, when just about everything seems funny, whether it is or not, that we can have some mighty good times.

If laughter is good medicine for the soul, deep belly laughs are the pot we may smoke.

I think I am finally beginning to understand that verse in scripture, "Unless a grain of wheat falls into the ground and dies, it cannot live."

Death ain't such a big ole thing if you have already died to live more fully and deeply and abundantly.

October 14

Boris Pasternak wrote of another, "He realized, more vividly than ever before, that art had two constant, two unending preoccupations: it is always meditating upon death and it is always thereby creating life."

There may be a thin line between tears and laughter. They are connected.

Tears may end as laughter begins or just the opposite may occur. They can even be simultaneous like sunshine and rain.

People tell me I am funny. I don't see it. My humor is so dry it could easily be described as an over-cooked turkey on Thanksgiving Day.

People also tell me they can't tell when I am being serious or humorous.

I would think that would be a quandary for fellow travelers, but just imagine what it's like for me when I can't tell the difference either. And maybe the truth is, a lot of things are serious and humorous at the same time.

October 15

Maybe laughter is the grease of grace that keeps the wheel going round and round.

And I will say, in all seriousness, the older I get, the more humorous life seems to be. Imagine going at full throttle all your life and suddenly having the remote control snatched out of your hands. I could throw a temper tantrum, but what good would that do? You laugh or cry. I choose to laugh.

We all know the therapeutic value of laughter. Laughter stretches muscles, burns calories, and produces a natural energy booster. Who couldn't stand to lose a few calories? I was far too serious for a good part of the journey. I wish I had laughed more; I am trying to make up for lost time now.

October 16

Laughter is an immediate vacation, a getaway from noise and nonsense.

Laughter lifts us. Laughter takes us. Laughter heals us.

Contagious among travelers, laughter is a most joyful sound along Grace Street.

Laughter brings people out of their homes and into the world.

Laughter brings people together. Laughter is the same in every language.

I must say, my recent brushes with mortality have certainly heightened my awareness of what will happen someday. It also has assisted me in considering some of the absurdities of life, the humor, and may I say it, the stupidity of some of the stuff I stress over. A good laugh will chase that stuff away.

October 17

Here's something that happened. I was standing by my kitchen window and thinking about death.

That's not morbid for a person of "a certain age." It's going to happen someday, ready or not, and in fact, one of the rules of St. Benedict is "to keep death daily before one's eyes."

I realize the often-awful and grievous nature of death.

Sometimes the pain through which people go is unrelenting and terribly sad to watch and to feel as observers ourselves.

I know those who are left behind go through long valleys of grief. Grieving the loss of someone we have loved is a long journey and stays with us in some measure till the day we take our turn at the door of death.

October 18

I am not minimizing in the least the dreadful sadness which often accompanies death when I tell you: as I stood by my kitchen window, the more I thought about my own death, the more I laughed. I laughed uncontrollably. I punched death in the nose and laughed some more. I said,

"You don't scare me. I got your number a long time ago. I will die someday, but you will not win."

I shadowboxed and punched the air with my fists and kept right on laughing.

I can only tell you what happened. I cannot explain it, nor will I ever negate what people who leave us and those of us who remain feel in the inner recesses of the heart when faced with death.

Well, who knows? That's probably not the way it will happen in my case, but wouldn't it be a great and marvelous thing to make the transition while laughing and reaching the other side with one glad and glorious hallelujah?

Wouldn't that be a good way to walk on home?

The writer said, "Death is swallowed up in victory."

There's an old Chinese proverb: "Enjoy yourself. It's later than you think." That's seriously funny.

October 19

If my hunch is right and everything is grace, death is grace too.

Charlie Brown says, "Someday we will all die, Snoopy." Snoopy replies, "True, but on all the other days, we will not."

I think those other days are worth the laughter and that even death itself, with all its pain, can be a "glory hallelujah" grace-filled time as the saints go marching home.

October 20

We are indelibly, unspeakably One.
—Jonathan Daniels

Is it possible to swim in the Dead Sea if one is traveling on Grace Street?

I will speculate that if the Dead Sea is a type of no-outlet, nor tributary, and only a dead-end street to the World House, the answer is "No."

It is all well and exceedingly good to experience grace, but when grace takes up residence in us or dawns on us, we begin to naturally flow in streams of humble service and recognition of the God in all of us. To put it more specifically, grace enlivens us to join hands in an ever-widening circle of mutuality for the whole world. Grace becomes the heart of service in a desperately needy world.

October 21

Grace builds bridges to each other. There are no walls between us, for we are one family under one God. We build whole systems of thought, theology, philosophy, and churchiness to divide ourselves from one another.

Unfortunately, we sometimes see life through a tribal lens that says, "*They* do not look, act, or believe like me. Therefore, *they* are inadequate. And since *they* are inadequate, I will set about to prove to *them* that they are wrong, defective, and without value and that *they* need to be like me."

And from this lens comes not only what is written about in our society—separateness, lack, guilt, and shame—but also our judgmental and condemnatory oratory. What we often call a "conversation" is nothing more than a rabid soliloquy or a diatribe.

October 22

Gordon Light keeps singing, "Draw the circle wide, draw the circle wide. No one stands alone; we'll stand side by side. Draw the circle wide, draw it wider still. Let this be our song! No one stands alone. Standing side by side, draw the circle, draw the circle wide!"

We would have it differently sometimes, wouldn't we if we were in charge? We might choose to foolishly divide ourselves up by race, creed, color, and religion, even more foolishly by our sexuality, which is of such little consequence in the larger scheme of things.

Years ago, Mama gave me a music box with a map of the world on it. It plays, "What the world needs now is love sweet love . . ." I play it often, as just another one of those remembrances of Mother and also to remember what matters.

Love matters. Love wins. Love always wins.

October 23

It seems simplistic, naïve in our crazy mixed-up world, and yes, I know, love is sometimes not so easy, but love is the only way to live on Grace Street, where grace flows easily like a gentle stream after the rain.

It was the greatest single lesson I learned in my college years. It did not come from a history book or a science book or a great novel. I learned that all people are pretty much the same, and I was really not so very different from anyone else when it came to tears and laughter.

Thomas Merton wrote, "The beginning of love is to let those we love be perfectly themselves, and not to twist them to fit our own image. Otherwise we love only the reflection of ourselves we find in them."

I don't know who, but somebody said, "Who we are is who everybody else is."

October 24

It took me a while to understand this foundational truth. I grew up thinking that some people were less, and sometimes I even considered myself to be less, but then I discovered we are all pretty much in the same boat navigating our individual journeys to Grace Street.

I raise a hearty "Amen" when Justin Welby, the archbishop of Canterbury, says, "Grace is the most beautiful word in the language of God—it means love given freely and without expectation of return."

More than anything else, grace is the act of showing love to anyone, anytime, anywhere. Grace requires no prerequisites before being given.

October 25

Grace demands no responses once it is shared. Grace is love with no strings attached. Grace is a free gift. Grace greases the wheels and helps us get on down the road into more and more grace. Grace opens doors. Condemnation closes doors.

There are audacious and revolutionary people who live outside the boundaries because there are no boundaries when it comes to grace. They think new thoughts, embrace the now, and live on the cutting edge of the immeasurable, no calculated depth of the river of grace which is always overflowing its banks.

October 26

Jim Wallis of *Sojourners* is such a man. I have followed his writings for more than forty years and have had the privilege of hearing him a couple of times at the Carter Center in Atlanta. He is a clarion voice when it comes to how we foolishly try to draw the circle narrower. He speaks of our unending bent to racism and white privilege. He says clearly, "The idol of whiteness has separated us from God."

Wallis says, "The United States of America was established as a white society, founded upon the near genocide of another race and then the enslavement of yet another."

How we deny, excuse, and rationalize the way we sometimes act. The color of my skin has nothing to do with the man I am. And let's get real: "Black Lives Matter" has nothing to do at all with "All Lives Matter."

There were a few voices in early America who said of Native Americans and Africans, "We cannot do this to people." Thus emerged the evil thought "We will say they aren't really human, or we will say they are partly human."

Thus the origins of the Black Lives Matter movement are precisely not about all lives, but about black lives.

October 27

I have demonstrated a couple of times on the steps of the state capital in Atlanta against the bigotry and prejudice that keeps rearing its ugly head against the LGBT community, of which I am proudly a part.

I have written a chapter in *Traveling on Grace Street* about my life as a gay man.

Appallingly, we may draw the circle narrower. This happens strangely and particularly in some religious circles. What a weird inversion of thought and living.

I will hold in my heart forever the words Greg Kirby wrote me about my being a gay man. They are words for all of us who are in the process of coming to the full realization of who we are.

It may have to do with sexuality, or for you it may be something else. Here's what my beloved friend said:

What a beautiful picture you paint with your words.

Only soul eyes can see rites of passage for the beauty they are meant to be. Cultural conditioning believes we need to be prepared to fight, and the soul knows we only need to discover our self, pure Divine Love.

This is a passage from fear to joy, from force to power, from war to peace, and from isolation into connection. This is what Jesus spoke so much about and so few understood. He spoke about our passage from death to life, and yet it took me so many years to understand that the passage he spoke of was nothing more than a turning inward to the freedom, joy, and peace I had always had and been. Turning inward to that Divine spark that is life itself, turning inward and knowing that all is as it is meant to be, and it is divinely perfect.

October 28

Greg Kirby continues,

Once I turned inward, I found soul eyes, and thus a passage from fear to joy took place. Of course, I had to go nowhere nor did I have to do anything. Rather, I only had to be still and know, see, and accept my true place in the Divine puzzle of love and life.

Over the past 10 years I have also gained a clearer understanding of how difficult your life, and the passage of so many who have followed a journey very similar to yours, must have been: to exist within a culture that holds so firmly and fearfully to concepts of "right" and "wrong"—such as one's sexual preference, religious beliefs, etc.—and to find yourself forcefully placed on the "wrong" side of the rule book; to have a desire that feels so natural to you and yet is deemed by the "cultural editors" as something condemned by God. And we both know that God would never condemn himself; the Divine spirit within each of us.

The passage you have made is from person to presence, from confusion to clarity, from outward seeking to inward seeking, from fear to love. Once this happens, one no longer sees themselves by the labels society has handed them. In fact, the labels simply disappear, and what is left is the Divine self, which is all there ever was: a self that is allowed to show up in the world as gay, straight, zebra, horse, or whatever else the social order may need to label the Divine self.

October 29

Greg Kirby concludes,

And when you pass over from person to presence, false self to true self, suddenly the labels no longer stick, as you are who you are.

You have courageously made a passage from bondage to freedom.

And your preferences no longer have value; they are just beautiful and magical part of who you are . . . Perfect!

Yes to a Rite of Passage being nothing more than a shift in perspective from no to yes, from force to power, from fear to love, from bondage to freedom, and from rejection to acceptance of all that is being all perfect pieces of the Divine mosaic.

Namaste, Greg

Oh, beloved fellow travelers, closets of any kind are often dark and confining. Why don't we open the door and walk out into the brightness of a new way of living?

October 30

I choose to share a journal entry of mine. It is the only time I have stood vigil at the execution of a person. It is a way of honoring the memory of Brandon Jones, who was put to death in a Georgia State Prison on February 3, 2016 --

Brandon Astor Jones died at 12:46 this morning.

In solidarity with fifteen other people who oppose the death penalty, I stood outside one of the state prisons for more than a six hour vigil.

None of us could live through such an experience without being touched to the core of our being. What incredible fellow-travelers there were in that circle who understand something of mercy in the depths of their beings.

Brandon Jones was just short of his seventy-third birthday, the oldest person on Death Row in Georgia where he spent the last thirty five years of his life in a hell hole. Supreme Court Justice Stephen Breyer has spoken of the "unconscionably long" time many older people spend on death row.

Sixty additional people are waiting to be put to death on Georgia's Death Row.

Brandon Jones fought his death in his last six minutes of life. Initially he closed his eyes; six minutes later, he opened his eyes, and after looking at a clock on the wall and looking in the direction of the man who prosecuted him thirty-five years ago, he closed his eyes and left the sufferings of this earth.

Somehow the ground beneath my feet in that place comes to mind.

I see the reality of the dirt of the earth, of Georgia, where vengeance still rears its ugly head.

October 31

My journal entry of the execution continues --

Desmond Tutu says, "To take a life when a life has been lost is revenge, not justice." I see the feet, the shoes of the men and women who stand vigil.

I see and I think I smell the Southern pines in the distance. I see a few stars in the sky before the clouds move in and the early evening turns to the dark of night.

You grieve and walk alone until a fellow traveler joins you in the night air, in a roped-off area, while guards stand watch in full armor with their dogs, and then you rejoin the little huddled group of strangers, now your sisters and brothers, and grieve together.

You remember none of us are free until all of us are free.

After it was all over, witnesses to the execution gathered. It all seemed so mournfully real, like a death in the family, and so it was and is.

I finally fell asleep exhausted sometime after four in the morning, and I pray I will never be the same again.

I wish I had been holding vigils with others on such nights in the earlier years of my journey. I will do so from now till I die. Just as we were leaving the execution, the wind kicked up, and a hard, cold rain fell in torrents, as if God in God's providence was grieving.

It will take a while to grieve the senseless death of Brandon Jones and to find my own voice to protest the hideous nature of the death penalty. I take comfort in believing beloved Brandon, my brother, was always love at the core of his being. The man is now in the Arms of Grace. Memory Eternal.

November 1

Naysayers, the caution-minded, bean counters, gatekeepers, guardians of a brand to the exclusion of a wider circle might as well jump into the water, because ultimately grace will flood us and force us to swim or at least float in a raft if we must, into the free-flowing river of grace.

I gladly embrace the life and words of Thomas Merton, Thich Nhat Hahn, Richard Rohr, Henri Nouwen, Martin Luther King, John Lewis, Wendell Berry, John Philip Newell, and so many others who were and are the personification of grace.

And let us not forget our teachers Jesus and Gandhi, who lived among us as suffering servants.

November 2

I cannot leave the subject of the circle without these magnificent words from Thomas Merton that speak to our divisive cultural environment if we will listen:

"Our real journey in this life is interior: it is a matter of growth, deepening, and an ever greater surrender to the creative action of love and grace in our hearts. Never was it more necessary for us to respond to that action. I pray that we may all do so. The deepest level of communication is not communication but communion. It is beyond words, it is beyond speech, and it is beyond concept. Not that we discover a new unity. We discover an older unity. My dear brothers, we are already one. But we imagine that we are not. And what we have to recover is our original unity. What we have to be is what we are."

May I be so bold to say what divides us could be healed if we heeded the words of Merton, for grace discovers us; we recognize our original unity was always love, and we begin to act out Grace with one another.

This moment, this moment we have been given. This is the moment to be grace.

November 3

Let me seek, then, the gift of silence, and poverty, and solitude, where everything I touch is turned into prayer: where the sky is my prayer, the birds are my prayer, the wind in the trees is my prayer, for God is in all."
-Thomas Merton

Is it possible that the most radical thing we do is meditate?

More than all our work and activity, is it possible that our greatest treasure is mined in prayer?

Name it what you will: contemplation, prayer, meditation, centering, listening, or waiting in silence.

Richard Rohr questions, "What else will lead us beyond words, endless theories, and the prison of the private self, aside from contemplation?"

We simply are called to cease our chattering minds and get quiet and breathe. It is the ancient way, and it is the way of busy contemporaries in our hurried worlds.

November 4

Our chattering minds feed our illusions and keep us from moving into deeper realms of communion.

We were made for stillness and solitude. We were made in love and for love and for the deepest intimacy with our Creator.

There are many ways to meditate because we are all different in the ways we choose to communicate. What works for me may not work for you.

Experiment with a path of meditation most natural to your environment and to who you are.

Here is a way I meditate out of my own life experience. It isn't complex or threatening. In fact, it is as simple and powerful as breathing in and breathing out and coming into a sense of mindfulness.

Whenever I am feeling anxious, I will close my eyes, taking a deep breath through my nose, letting it gently fall out of the mouth.

After doing this two or three times, bring attention to the body. Notice the entire body: any aches, pains, place of relaxation, warm or cool spots. Sit with your body as an observer, not judging or intending; just notice it.

After a period of sitting with your body, move your attention to your breath. Notice the depth, strength, weakness of your breath . . . just notice your breathing for a time. Be an observer.

Next, move your attention to your mind: noticing what's there, remembering not to judge anything; just notice. Next, bring your attention back to your body and begin to fill each part with thankfulness.

Allow the white light of thankfulness to fill each part of your body. Sit with thankfulness for a time, noticing how light and joyful it is. Take a deep breath through your nose into your diaphragm and gently let it fall from your mouth.

Slowly open your eyes. Peace to you.

November 5

Maybe begin with five minutes in your chosen place of comfort. Maybe begin in a chair, or at a desk, or in your backyard, or in the woods, or in the parking lot of a busy shopping center. It doesn't matter as much where you begin as it matters that you begin.

In your breathing in and out, you may choose a personal mantra. One of the ones I use is "Be still and know," as I breathe in and, "that I am God," as I breathe out. Invariably, even the breathing in and out slowly and deliberating puts me into a place of peace and connection.

It's most often my mantra when I am anxious at the hospital or about some other circumstance.

November 6

We may experience God in the fire, or in a burning bush, or in the love of a partner or a child or a fellow traveler. We may experience Presence in a sunset or sunrise, a bird that sings outside our window, a good book, a walk in the woods, or a multiplicity of other places and ways. The important thing is to pay attention and to be aware.

We need not go off on a long search for God or Presence because Presence is as close as our hearts, as near as the breath we breathe.

As we breathe in and out, we begin to listen and to come into Presence.

November 7

As my prayer life has evolved, prayer isn't so much about words. In fact, the fewer words from me, the better. Prayer is about listening. We listen with our hearts, not with chattering minds.

I remember a college student who told me one day of a discovery he had made. He said, "I am learning that God speaks to me mostly in silence." At a relatively young age, he had learned one of the great secrets of the mystics.

The monks teach us likewise. The Psalmist said, "Wait," and the Psalmist has God saying, "Be still and know that I am God."

November 8

Oh the preciousness, the beauty of spending a sweet hour in prayer or five minutes of breathing a single prayer of one word many times a day and into the night.

However, the truth is that sometimes we hardly feel the need of prayer. We have food to eat, a shelter over our heads, clothes to wear, and everything we think we need; but we need so much more than the temporal, the fleeting stuff of life. And we are a busy people.

A fellow traveler asked me to join a virtual group on the Internet called "The Office" to pray three times a day through a community in Scotland.

We laughed, however, when we said it would have to be next week because we were too busy with other stuff this week. And so it is in our hectic lives.

November 9

I treasure E. Stanley Jones's words in his thin paperback, *Prayer Is Surrender.* What a definition. What a way to see meditation. What a way of opening our hands, palms up in surrender, not with clenched fists or telling God what we want God to do, but empty handed and available to the great mystery of love in each of our hearts.

Anne Lamott has a wonderful little book where she writes about the three essential prayers: *Help, Thanks, Wow.*

Maybe we just say Yes when we pray, and maybe that single word is enough, more than enough, and everything.

Prayer is Yes to God, to ourselves, and to others.

November 10

I like the way Frederick Buechner describes our dilemma: "The original, shimmering self gets buried so deep that most of us end up hardly living out of it at all. Instead we live out of all the other selves, which we are constantly putting on and taking off like coats and hats against the world's weather."

Before God, we may take off our coats and hats and put them away. We may stand naked in God's Presence where there are no secrets. That is the intimacy we may experience.

Sometimes I become centered by walking out into the starry night like I did when I was a boy.

November 11

I remember lying on my back in a grassy field and under the canopy of heaven. I remember considering the vast expanse of the creation and how small I felt and how great God is.

It's like that on so many early mornings now, just at daybreak.

I walk out to breathe the early air, observe the Morning Star, and the moon sometimes whispers, "Good morning. I love you. Look for the sunrise over behind the Southern short-leafed pines, and I will see you again tonight."

Is not this the communion where there is no need for words?

A little brush with mortality has a way of resetting priorities.

It's all a loving reminder that we are here to seize every moment we are given. I say given because, truth be told, I don't earn anything. It's all a gift. Everything is given.

November 12

Grace became my life word a few years back, and it will suit me just fine if the last word I speak earth-side is grace.

Even as I write these words, I hear the birds singing their hearts out.

That's it! That's the secret. Heart to heart.

Grace is heart to heart.

November 13

Do not grow old, no matter how long you live. Never
cease to stand like curious children before the
Great Mystery into which we are born.
-Albert Einstein

We see Love when our lens is clean.

We see with Thomas Merton: "Grace is the immutable diamond blazing in the heart."

When I met Kathleen Singh of Florida, who has written extensively on the subject of grace, I saw through her lens when she said, "Grace is the most meaningful word in my life. I go for refuge to God for grace."

I find myself seeing in new ways. Former things have passed away.

Those old ghosts of the past raise their heads on occasion, but I am by and large done with them. They have no hold on me.

Awakening, not activity, is the key to enlightenment.

November 14

I sense the scales are falling off my eyes. Not that I always see clearly, for as Paul, the Apostle said, "Now we see through a glass darkly. Someday we will see clearly." But things are clear enough to make me feel more than a conqueror, not of my doing, but because of Love's bidding. Love bats last.

Love always wins. Everything else will crumble away, but Love holds steady in the boat. It's just like that on Grace Street.

Maybe it began when those fractures started to show up. Living with fractures invariably opens us to places we have never traveled.

Maybe it was my digging around in the soil of grace for several years.

Maybe it was you in my life, fellow travelers.

Maybe the threads of love simply came together in a moment, and life took on new meaning and discovery.

November 15

I sense something has begun to change in me, and I am beginning to see in new ways. How long will it last? I hope to the grave and beyond. I have a hunch it's about letting go and not hanging on. I believe it has to do with the discovery of what was already within me from my beginnings.

I am learning not to beg or plead or go off on a long search. I don't even need to open my hands to receive because Love was, and is, and always will be in my heart. I only need to accept and appropriate the Love which has always been. For me, that's grace. That's Presence.

That's who we all are. It's the way we were made. It's the Love that we are. All of us. It's just the way we may choose to roll.

November 16

Everything for us is not always sunshine and roses. There are those thorns, those prickly and brittle and pesky things, that stuff, which keeps us down close to the ground where we belong and from which we may grow.

Did the Teacher not say, "Unless a grain of wheat falls into the ground and dies, it cannot live."

I sense that may be the secret to having our lens clean.
I sense the chattering mind never leads to clear vision. I know the ego blurs the vision. I know Love clarifies and focuses the vision.

November 17

I sense we must sit together at a roundtable as the people of the earth if we are to see and to embrace the challenges of our time.

I sense the old wineskins just will not work anymore in religion and that we might as well strip ourselves down to the essentials like doing justice, loving mercy, and walking humbly with God. Maybe it's past time to get back to the original intent of all the great religions of the world: loving God and loving our neighbor.

Through my lens, I cannot see the future, but I know who holds me in the future, and I know God's name is Grace, everything is grace, and grace is the immutable diamond blazing in the sun.

November 18

I have learned on Grace Street that the anchors hold. No matter how much the winds beat upon the house and the storms come, the foundation of Love does not crumble.

I have learned that what Mother Teresa said is true: "The most terrible poverty is loneliness, and the feeling of being unloved."

I saw Mother Teresa once when I was in my early forties, and I will never forget the moment.

She was small in stature, yet to be near her was to be in the awesome presence of Love. She spoke simply and directly. There was no guile or pretense. Only love.

She lived a poured-out life for others and knew her own loneliness.

She did not run from the realities of human existence; rather, she embraced it all—the light and darkness, the pain and suffering, the poverty and immense depth of richness which was her spirit. She had nothing. She had everything.

November 19

Truth is, we have everything.

Everything within us, as Richard Rohr reminds us, "Your True Self is who you are, and always have been in God; and at its core, it is love itself. Love is both who you are and who you are still becoming, like a sunflower seed that becomes its own sunflower . . . There's nothing you can do to make God love you more; and there's nothing you can do to make God love you less. All you can do is nurture your True Self, which is saying quite a lot. It is love becoming love in this unique form called 'me.'"

Don't you dare believe the lies people will tell you about yourself.

Don't you dare believe you are whatever you have done in the past or will do in the future.

Do not believe you are anything but Love.

November 20

Greg Kirby says, "The journey—experienced through a lens of love—brings us into a place of spaciousness and peace as we make our way along this stream (path) of love. And while in this place of spaciousness and peace, the arms of our soul spread wide, accepting everything just as it is, including ourselves. We then begin to melt together just as a drop of water becomes one with the ocean—from which it came in the first place—into the oneness of it all."

November 21

Rumi puts it like this, "I have come to drag you out of yourself and take you in my heart. I have come to bring out the beauty you never knew you had and lift you like a prayer to the sky."

And, oh the power of the words of Ezra Bayda when it comes to whatever the circumstances of life send us: "When you really pay attention, everything is your teacher."

Here's what is happening in my journey as I learn to pay attention with everything as my teacher.

I have a growing awareness of a deep sense of praise welling up in my heart.

It strikes me unexpectedly, like I just want to drop to my knees and offers up a word of praise.

It's gratitude and more. It's an overflowing measure of praise that flies in the face of circumstances.

November 22

I have no idea how to explain or articulate the moment because I sense it has little to do with me.

Maybe it has origins in surrender. Maybe it is the palatable mindfulness of Love. Maybe it is the support of people who care.

Maybe it is the reaching out to others in their times of need.

Maybe it is shedding some of the old weights which have encumbered my journey. Shedding old skins and drinking New Wine are joyful things.

I sense authenticity, with nothing to hide or be ashamed of; no condemnation, bedrock honesty. I'll embrace it, accept it as a gift, a gift of grace.

I only know I am in the Presence of Love, and this presence seems more than enough, overflowing like a stream in spring after winter.

November 23

Very rarely in my life have I felt forsaken. And it seems the harder the times, the greater the Presence.

Let me be clear: I have known fractures, hard places, depression, loneliness, and unfaithfulness, but I look back and see how the thread of the faithfulness of Love has been weaving its way all along the journey. It was never about me.

Grace is always about God.

November 24

I remember a conversation I had with Owen, my grandson, when he was a young lad.

I asked Owen where God is and what God looks like. "Well," he said with certainty, "God's in heaven, and God has a long beard."

"I think God's in heaven," I affirmed, "but here on earth too."

"Is God's beard white?" I inquired. "No, it's brown," he was sure.

"Granddaddy, are you a hundred years old?"

"No, grandson, not yet."

Not yet. If we live in the now and keep our lens clean, the "not yet" will take care of itself.

Here's what I see through my lens: Love is a never-ending circle of heaven and earth, and Thomas Merton was right when he said, "The gate of heaven is everywhere."

November 25

I enjoy planting pansies before winter comes on.

Pansies speak to me of a simple beauty, perseverance and an endurance in winter. I find them healing on cold grey days.

I had twenty plants and carelessly broke the roots off one of them -- a reminder to be careful if handling in any way the roots of another -- a child or marginalized person.

Every spade into the dirt became a prayer -- a prayer of faith, hope, love. And the greatest of these is love.

November 26

We all have moments
— fleeting, brief when the noise vanishes and the stone is rolled away. Deep breaths of oneness — perfect harmony with creation as we return to who we are.

One was given to me just at dusk in these ancient mountains of North Carolina, the oldest mountains in the world.

A late autumn chill awakened all my senses as I walked in silence.

No striving. No anxiousness. No clutter. Oneness.

November 27

I've always had wanderlust. Wonder too though I don't travel as much as I used to. It's a pity for I'm like a kid on Christmas morning when it comes to going places, seeing people.

Every common place, every- day ordinary places take on a joy all their own.

Every fellow-traveler I encounter becomes extraordinary because I know they have a story to tell -- something to teach me -- There's a spark and I'm never quite the same again.

November 28

You only lose what you cling to. – Buddha

November 29

I love the days we celebrate the saints of all the ages.

Surrounded by the saints of all the ages, living and gone on and living still. A great cloud of witnesses. A mighty chorus.

Buffering us, carrying us on their shoulders. Never really far from us. I feel their presence -- their palatable presence -- and I am lifted by their lives, words, deeds.

No need to tell me that when we die it's over or that's all there is. No sir. On and on we live with the saints of all the ages. A glorious origin and destiny while the ages roll.

God, I can see them. The ones in my life who nurtured me: mama, grandparents, kin not always blood kin, mostly not blood kin. Fellow travelers, friends. Writers and poets, advocates for justice. Salt, light, anchors, lighthouses.

Women and men who had some backbone, who knew how to sweat and swear, counted the cost and went on ahead anyway.

'Wind of the North
Grandmother, Grandfather
Hummingbird, Ancestor
We honor you who have come before and
You who are yet to come."
 - Dylan James Bryne

What company. Communion, mystic sweet communion.

Don't you think for one moment that our being is any less than extraordinary in such company. All saints. All of us. Salty human broken soaring saints. Every one of us a saint. Glory be.

November 30

"You've got to know when to hold 'em
Know when to fold 'em /Know when to walk away
And know when to run. "
- Kenny Rogers, The Gambler lyrics

It's hard to know sometimes. I mean you want to be civil, even kind, but you also want to tell your truth as you know your truth or what you believe to be truth.

But everybody's truth is different. And sometimes an individual's truth may sound pretty strange or harsh to the sensitive ears of somebody else.

You realized a long time ago that you do not speak from a position of superiority, moral or otherwise, but you do have a mind and a heart and a voice.

I really don't know where some characterizations of Jesus come from. You would think Jesus never turned the tables in the temple or referred to some people as vipers and snakes.

Jesus was no Peace Child with flowers in his hair. He said, "Do not suppose that I have come to bring peace to the earth. I did not come to bring peace, but a sword."

A sword? I thought he was a peacemaker and I thought I was a pacifist.

If only Community was so easy. If only we just needed priests and no prophets in the world.

Pope Francis said, "Make trouble."

John Lewis said, "You must find a way to get in the way and get in good trouble, necessary trouble."

The hour is late. The barbarians are at the gate. Stay in the arena and in the battle until we realize we really do need each other and we will never get to where we've got to go without bearing with, listening to, speaking up, which is to say, stirring the pot.

December 1

I was listening to a Choral Evensong from Westminster Abbey on BBC 3.

The worship was a commemoration of the centenary of the birth and later the martyrdom of Oscar Romero.

I was made to give thanks for women and men of courage who have shown us the way by their faithfulness and fearlessness in the face of great obstacles.

Challenges between good and evil like we are locked in just now.

Faithfulness and fearlessness always come at a cost.

Rowan Williams, former Archbishop of Canterbury, gave the homily and told a little story of two Welshmen, I believe they were, who were having a drink and a conversation in a pub about the death of someone they knew.

"What did he leave?" asked one. "Everything," said the other.

Everything – When we die, we will leave . . . everything.

The days are swiftly passing. Hold nothing back. Leave it all on the field of this given life.

Everything.

December 2

The spirituality I have been exposed to in recent years has given me a new way of seeing and living.

To be human is to experience a multiplicity of emotions and to know there are from time to time, no easy answers -- nor should there necessarily be.

We are sometimes left with realities which bring us to our knees.

For most of my seventy years, I have been able to find a way to walk around or climb over whatever obstacle was in the path.

In the good providence of God, there was a way -- a way through the wilderness and I still often walk that path with much gratitude.

But the fractures of the journey are teaching me not to run or flee (my natural inclination), but to stand in place or fall to my knees and to discover whatever it is I'm being taught.

Do I believe grace is everywhere or not? I believe grace is everywhere.

Parker Palmer, the Quaker, is one of those who has taught me not to run but to name, acknowledge, embrace. Kathleen Singh, our beloved who left us not even a month ago, with her profound Buddhist leanings, is another.

I was grieving over matters out of my control and Katrina Harper, a beloved friend, came to my rescue with some incarnational suffering-with-love and gut level reality.

She wrote, "I keep starting to write and deleting. And starting again and then deleting again. Words are ringing like clanging bells right in this moment. The simple truth is this - I am with you. With you in this grief. With you in this pain. Adding my heart to yours and lifting up all the questions and longings that go with it . . . to be soothed this night with love and ease . . . with the only things we know for sure. We are here, we are here for each other, and we are loved."

December 3

So I'm sitting here in my car on a lovely sunlit day.

Tears are streaming down my face.

I've just read something my beloved friend Chris Weidner posted,

"If we walk with those who have been the most crushed, then something will happen within us. I call you to take seriously how beautiful you are, even with all your wounds and weaknesses and the call to honour those who are the weakest." (Jean Vanier, Encountering the Other)

December 4

It is a beautiful thing when the center holds.

- Jeannie Waller Harper

This journey we're on will do a number on us.

We're not around long before we realize life is both lovely and sometimes terrorizing.

I've given up on the idea that I can just sail right through it all, unscathed and unscarred -- a model of perfect peace and tranquility. Some days I'm rattled.

There's this culture all around us that will suck us into its mold -- swallow us whole and then spit us out.

I can only tell you my experience. Finding a place to retreat from it all -- to run and hide -- yes a hiding place -- is the only way to engage, stay in the fray, bring a little sanity to the insanity we encounter when our eyes are wide open and we wake up to life as it is.

May I call it meditation? Mindfulness. A place where we are accepted. Here's a place where there is no resistance to the Yes of Love, the Yes of Grace. We don't have to grab or grasp.

Isn't it a beautiful thing when the center holds?

December 5

"So it has been a bit of a struggle" just yesterday writes a fellow-traveler -- and "The tough call is when to say Uncle."

We get it don't we? This journey is breath-taking beautiful yet sometimes an immense struggle. We taste the bitterness of loneliness, anxiety, fear, depression and wonder how to go on, to keep walking,

Relationships test our stamina. It is from time to time exasperating to bear with each other, to build bridges instead of walls.

This week I have been reading Corey Taylor's book, "Dying - a memoir." It's the story of a woman who is dying of melanoma cancer and how she copes with each passing day.

We are told to consider our mortality every day which is not a morbid introspection rather a way to suck the marrow out of every precious moment we are given

The dynamics of fear and hope, faith and doubt, love and hate, test us and I have learned that avoidance is not the answer.

I'm not sure there is any way around it which means we go through it. Don't run. Stay in the fray, the midst of it.

The fire will burn the dross away. Time down at the Potter's House is the way to get through -- maybe even with some abundance of courage and strength for the journey.

My hero for such matters is one of my grandchildren who faces repeated obstacles and keeps on going.

He's my namesake, young AJ, a great light on my path.

December 6

There are so many ways we experience healing.

In mystery, I do not always understand how the human family is susceptible to illness, invasions of disease and sickness.

I do know in my own life, I am after a holistic approach, integrative medicine for the healing of my body, mind and soul.

We are sometimes brought to our knees and often most of us encounter obstacles or fractures in our physical well-being somewhere along the way.

We long for healing, wholeness and the good news is there are multiplicities of ways we may heal.

December 7

We have healing places and there are people all along the way who are instruments of healing. After all the medicines, the surgeries, the pokes and prods, there is nothing more healing than the love and nurture of people who walk beside us every step of the way.

I am well blessed to have several instruments of healing in my life including Trina Ford, my health coach, who has made such a difference in my journey.

We talk often about practical ways we heal, like walking and other simple exercises, as well as staying socially connected to people.

Reading and writing are so therapeutic in my life as well as meditation -- mindfulness.

It is not the past or the future but the now where we live and where the fears that so easily beset us are laid aside in quietness and stillness and the focus of the heart thrives on the healing balms of love.

Trina has helped me focus on 7 Attitudes of Mindfulness:

Non-judgement
Patience
Beginner's mind
Trust
Non-striving
Acceptance
Letting go
(Jon Kabatt-Zinn MD -- Full Catastrophe Living)

December 8

We pray the Metta Prayer:

> May you be happy
> May you be healthy
> May you be safe
> May you live with ease

Will I be healed? Will you be healed? Will the people we care about be healed?

I believe the answer is yes.

It may not be in the precise physical ways that we hope but we are being healed in even deeper ways than we can understand or imagine or that may be measured with human instrumentality for we are so very much more than our bodies. So very much more.

December 9

Bill Laramee, a fellow-traveler with roots in Vermont, sent me the words of Rabbi Naomi Levy -- just about the most heart-pumpin' words I've ever read on the subject of grace --

"Sometimes something breaks through to you...Suddenly the lesson you need to hear isn't just washing over you — it hits you deeply . . . The rabbis describe these times as moments of grace. In Hebrew this opening is called Et Ratzon, a time of wanting and being wanted, when your longing is met by a divine longing. It is a spiritual time when doors that are normally locked are open. A time when we're given the vision to see our lives through a wider lens, to hold things in perspective. To see the truth we've been hiding from. It's a time when opposite poles fall into alignment. When the human desire to reach upward is met with the divine desire to reach out. When the soul's desire to repair the world is met with the body's desire to act . . . Hold on to it {GRACE} for dear life and don't let it slip away. Notice it, welcome it, allow it to leave a lasting imprint on your life so that it becomes, in the words of Song of Songs, 'a seal upon your heart . . . A moment of grace can evaporate like mist or it can lead to lasting change."

December 10

Daybreak in Alabama

When I get to be a composer
I'm gonna write me some music about
Daybreak in Alabama
And I'm gonna put the purtiest songs in it
Rising out of the ground like a swamp mist
And falling out of heaven like soft dew.
I'm gonna put some tall tall trees in it
And the scent of pine needles
And the smell of red clay after rain
And long red necks
And poppy colored faces
And big brown arms
And the field daisy eyes
Of black and white black white black people
And I'm gonna put white hands
And black hands and brown and yellow hands
And red clay earth hands in it
Touching everybody with kind fingers
And touching each other natural as dew
In that dawn of music when I
Get to be a composer
And write about daybreak
In Alabama.

by Langston Hughes

December 11

There is that delightful exchange between Bill Moyers and Wendell Berry on contrariness that I go back to from time to time just to remind myself to keep rockin' the boat and stirrin' the pot at least every now and then:

Bill Moyers:

You've got to be contrary."

Wendell Berry:

"Well, you've got to be contrary, but there's a world of pleasure in contrariness.

'Dance,' they told me, and I stood still, and while they stood quiet in line at the gate of the Kingdom, I danced. 'Pray,' they said, and I laughed, covering myself in the earth's brightnesses, and then stole off gray into the midst of a revel, and prayed like an orphan. When they said, 'I know that my Redeemer liveth,' I told them, 'He's dead.' And when they told me, 'God is dead,' I answered, 'He goes fishing every day in the Kentucky River.' I see him often . . . Going against men, I've heard at times a deep harmony thrumming in the mixture, and when they asked me what I say I don't know. It is not the only or the easiest way to come to the truth. It is one way."

December 12

The Buddha said the greatest of all teachings is impermanence. Its final expression is death. -Judy Lief in "Lion's Roar"

A brush with mortality or the awareness of death at the door is a great teacher, the greatest teacher, and maybe the secret to life.

We may choose to fight it, deny it, or accept it.

Regardless, it is coming as sure as the changing seasons, the beautiful falling leaves of autumn. There is a time to be born and a time to die.

Illness will bring us to our knees and force us, ready or not, to deal with life's most urgent questions.

Nothing may go as planned or hoped for and nothing is nailed down. We might as well drop the mic, the remote control, and as one fellow traveler said this week, discover that we are not in control after all.

December 13

Impermanence is in many ways, a fearful thing and yet, and yet, has the potential to be transformative -- our ultimate liberation for "unless a grain of wheat falls into the ground and dies, it cannot live." It's the paradox, the irony, the letting go.

I am sometimes like the last leaf on the tree in late fall, hanging on instead of letting when I know if i just let go, I will be carried on the gentle breeze to freedom.

It's the great lesson I have learned from monasticism and why I return to the monastery over and over again.

The monks teach me how to get into the flow of the journey, when to hang on and when to let go in the constant movement of the hours, day and night.

As I write these words in the deepest part of the night, I look around the room where I am. I see symbols of the various stages of my journey. I see photographs of people I love and who love me.

The room tells a story of what might appear to be permanence but that is an illusion for nothing is nailed down and everything is changing.

It's getting into the music of impermanence where we learn to dance through the night into the morning. I think that's Grace.

December 14

The only thing separating you from grace are all your beliefs.

\- Kathleen Singh

The death of beloved Kathleen Singh weighed heavy on our hearts. She was a teacher and practitioner of grace, a friend and fellow-traveler for so many of us in the school, the laboratory of lived out grace

Grace is such a beautiful gift, experience -- I wonder sometimes why we fight it -- why we have such a time with falling into the arms of grace -- trusting -- surrendering -- resting - being still.

December 15

Providentially, Kathleen Singh had another new book out in the week of her death - *Unbinding: The Grace Beyond Self* and I think she comes as close as ever to answering the question as to why we struggle with grace. I invite you to hear her profound words:

"I woke up abruptly one morning with these words echoing in my mind: 'The only thing separating you from grace are all of your beliefs.' In that moment, I realized—with an almost physical shock—that my most foundational, oft-repeated belief was the belief that I exist in the way I imagine myself to exist and that that belief pervaded every conception, emotion, perception, action, reaction, and relationship. Buddha compared the consequences of this belief to 'tangled reeds.' That was my experience—a flash of a vision of how deep-rooted and entangling are self's tentacles—a snarled swirl of hurts and how obstructive.

It was a big moment, a moment of real transformative shift. It led me to the helpful habit of labeling all tightness, all minds of turmoil, all self-reference as 'ignorance.' Using that blanket word to name unease has kept me from tumbling into my ordinary explanations or justifications of the unease. Just labeling the unease as 'ignorance' has greatly enabled my practice of surrender. This informal practice drops us out of conceptual mind, the home of self and ignorance, directly into the heart."

Our beloved lived from moment to moment and now she knows the ultimate unbinding grace.

December 16

I wake myself up singing around four o'clock this morning,

> "We're marching to Zion,
> Beautiful, beautiful Zion;
> We're marching upward to Zion,
> The beautiful city of God."

The house is dark and quiet -- yet there is a sense of light, the sweet harmony before the sure knowledge the morning comes soon enough.

The nations of the world meet at the United Nations in New York this week against the ominous threat to wipe one nation off the face of the Earth.

We are like barbarians and nomads in an alien land -- yet joining the Singer in asking how we shall sing God's song in a strange land where we know we are just passing through.

Weighted down by too much burden to bear, uncertain of what new fracture will threaten our equilibrium and remind us of our impermanence and fragility.

Our brothers and sisters in slavery keep singing in the fields, reminding us to keep our eye on the prize. They will not, they could not, bear these burdens alone and neither should we.

We're marching to Zion. Beautiful, beautiful Zion.

December 17

New truths are emerging all the time. -Ken Wilbur

Those early perceptions we acquire when it comes to religion are sometimes washed away like the sand on the beaches in the Florida Keys.

A whole lot we are culturally conditioned to believe primarily because of birth or geography, turns out to be pretty much a crock, to put it in a nice way. Good riddance.

What we swallowed may have served a purpose in adolescence, but it doesn't cut it when the hard realities and unrelenting questions of the long journey emerge.

I say it is no wonder we are living in a post-Christian western world and that the culture is increasingly secular -- whatever secular means.

A lot of what I hear and read makes me extremely angry and tempted to call the whole thing off except . . . I sense there is something more.

December 18

I identify with Bruce Michael Douville, fellow traveler, when he writes, "I've spent years studying religion -- both academically and personally. And I both *get it* and "don't get it.* But it's still fun, and funny, and sometimes, deeply meaningful (and sometimes, all three at the same time)."

I find it virtually impossible to figure most of it out and maybe the fact that it is all so much bigger than me, is a good thing. So many questions, so few answers, though I do not wish to miss whatever the spirit is saying and wherever the spirit is leading.

What Ken Wilbur says, moves me. I want to be open to new truths, new understandings of what the spirit is saying.

I can only embrace my own little corner of it all and count most of it mystery, a Transcendence so infinitely greater than me.

It just seems to me we could use a whole new kind of humility -- with whatever there is that is greater and certainly with each other.

I know so little and I can only bow down to the ground and ask for grace to make it the rest of the way home.

December 19

My friend Mark Herman shares these words from Erin Van Vuren.

The profundity blows me away.

We face watershed moments that have the potential to make us better, times when we find the strength and courage to keep going in spite of it all.

Call it grace or love or God or whatever you choose, it's there.

As present as the air we breathe. And isn't it beautiful? How we are carried on the wings of the morning.

There are forces at work that will seek to conform us to a lesser path that will attempt to squeeze us into its mold.

Robert Frost wrote,

> "I shall be telling this with a sigh
> Somewhere ages and ages hence:
> Two roads diverged in a wood, and I—
> I took the one less traveled by,
> And that has made all the difference."

Van Vuren says, "But don't you go and become something that you aren't."

And, keep moving!

December 20

It seems like a good day to reset the compass.

The storm came, the wind blew, the house shook but did not fall because the foundation was and is solid.

You likely know what I mean.

Grace was and is and always will be greater.

Greater than what? Well certainly greater than me.

Greater than the sum of any high mountain or low valley.

Greater than the hardest question. The deepest doubt.

Grace is greater because there is now and never was, any condemnation.

There was not or will there ever be, any separation.

Grace is greater than whether we live or die because grace is everywhere.

December 21

Just to be is a blessing. Just to live is holy. -Abraham Hershel

I keep these words above my desk as a reminder of the privilege we have every day to be a blessing in the lives of each other.

I often set as a goal, an offering of some blessing to ten people before eight in the morning -- some word, some connection, and some way of loving more fully. I suppose it sounds rather arbitrary, but, I like the discipline, the intentional nature of it all.

We need not go off to a monastery to live holy lives for as Hershel reminds us, "Just to live is holy." To breathe. To be. To love and be loved in all our humanity, broken as it is sometimes.

Rilke said, "Being here is so much . . . "

December 22

Today is full of opportunity. A well-focused and healing hour-long conversation with a fellow-traveler about my age in Belgium was edifying. It's like that when we are open and vulnerable with each other.

A younger brother reminded me of his appreciation for shared humanity. That too is the stuff of holiness.

A younger sister shared the jarring news of a cancer diagnosis and I responded as best I could, "I know this fracture comes to you as unsettling and a challenge. How we need around us people who care and love and stay. So much of the journey comes as a surprise and I don't exactly know why, but it does, and somehow we find ways to go on with it all. Your foundation, now shaking, is firm and as you say, it is what it is. As the Quakers say, 'I am holding you in the Light.'"

Grace is holding each other in the Light.

December 23

Five times a day the monks at the monastery gather beginning at 4:00 am Vigils and concluding at 7:30 pm Compline or Night Prayer.

Compline is a beautiful liturgy of prayer and even when the days are shorter, the same prayers are sung every night in the dark.

I take it to be a kind of letting go or surrender as the day ends and night comes on.

As some days go on, there were moments when my heart is troubled.

I find comfort and no small measure of courage in knowing the monks, and millions of people, pray all the time.

I read and now recite from memory every night, Jane Kenyon's poem, "Let Evening Come" which prompts me to imagine that she heard monks in some monastery singing Compline in the night.

December 24

Every dark night is met eventually by a new morning. Let us all be bringers of the dawn. -Marianne Williamson

Isn't that beautiful? True too. Reminds me of the psalmist who said, "Weeping may endure for a night but joy comes in the morning."

There is plenty of night out there. We all know people who are suffering unimaginably and facing the realities of life head-on. It may be physical or mental or emotional, but it is real. The wounds are there.

We say to take care of it all, there is the need to live in the Now, in the moment, and that is true, but the realities are unrelenting. Beyond the mind, the heart knows the wounds are there.

I think to be a bringer of the morning is to be well acquainted with the night but not overcome by it.

It is to embrace those who are in pain and to walk quietly beside them with stubborn courage.

It is to love with a greater love than we have yet known.

We measure it out don't we? We say we have loved enough, more than enough and we have done our part.

And we say we have loved as fully as we can and I say no we have not. There is still a deeper place of being which cannot be measured as we plumb the depths of love.

It is to keep going to the ground of our being and to experience a tenacious love found deep within us that knows no limit.

Let us be bringers of the morning to those we love and cherish and to as many other fellow-travelers as we are able, for there is no night so dark but the morning comes.

December 25

And his name shall be called
Wonderful
Counselor
The Mighty God
The Everlasting Father
The Prince of Peace

Isaiah 9:6

December 26

We struggle with paradox, the seeming contradictions of the journey.

We are full of faith and we doubt. We fear and hope. We love and sometimes find it difficult to love. We are healthy and whole, fractured and broken. We see and are blind. We hear and are deaf.

To be able to hold in creative tension the contradictions is not hypocrisy but honesty, not weakness but strength, a stubborn questioning while we are being made and remade without the duality which can easily overtake us.

Is that a grimace or a smile? Are we awake or sleeping?

Satisfied or so very hungry for more? Full or running on empty?

We are flesh and blood mortality. We are spirit and mystery.

We are made a little lower than the angels with enormous capacity to do good yet we sometimes do evil to ourselves and others.

We are star dust. Like the stars in the heavens.

The cremated remains of an adult male weigh about 6 pounds and the remains of a female weigh about 4 pounds. Ashes to ashes. Dust to dust. Vanity of vanities, all is vanity. That's us.

Every single one of us is a spiritual entity, made for something more, something or someone greater than ourselves with the capacity to choose our destiny in the stuff of real life.

I believe we are never more spiritual than when we are fully human, embracing the seeming paradox, the irony, our imperfections, the not yet places on our journey of being and becoming.

December 27

You do not need to know precisely what is happening, or exactly where it is all going. What you need is to recognize the possibilities and challenges offered by the present moment, and to embrace them with courage, faith, and hope. -Thomas Merton

But I always wanted a road map of my own design.

You know --- straight paths, easy climbs over mountains, tranquil country roads with a swimming hole to skinny dip, a pleasant inn by the side of the road to rest at night.

Except -- except that's not always the highway we are given. Life sometimes gets in the way of my intentions and things happen we never could have imagined.

It's learning to travel sometimes without a roadmap, particularly one of my making that potentially makes all the difference in the world.

There are signs everywhere which read 'possibilities' and 'challenges' and frankly I can get pretty lost if I do not remember the map maker who in ways I could never imagine is preparing a path.

I can trust the map maker even without a map in hand.

December 28

Most of my life I didn't quite get Thomas Merton's prayer because I mistakenly thought I had a pretty good idea how the journey would unfold.

Only in recent years have I faced some uncertainties and sometimes felt like a lost and lonely child, like the day my mother died, and Merton's prayer has begun to come alive.

My Lord God,
I have no idea where I am going.
I do not see the road ahead of me.
I cannot know for certain where it will end.
Nor do I really know myself,
and the fact that I think that I am following Your will
does not mean that I am actually doing so.
But I believe that the desire to please You
does in fact please You.
And I hope that I have that desire
in all that I am doing.
And I know that if I do this,
You will lead me by the right road
although I may know nothing about it.
Therefore will I trust You always,
though I may seem to be lost
and in the shadow of death,
I will not fear, for You are ever with me,
and will never leave me
to face my perils alone. -Thomas Merton

We go on -- led by the Unseen Hand of Grace.

December 29

There is more faith in honest doubt than in all the creeds of the church. --Leslie Weatherhead

I sat late in the week with a fellow-traveler who I deeply respect and with whom I have shared conversations for a number of years.

Our talk quite naturally turned to spirituality.

I know the depths of her long journey now into her 80s as a leader in her church and I appreciate her impeccable integrity.

She questioned, with refreshing wisdom and discernment, this matter of spirituality.

She said, "Did we make it all up?"

I laughed. I like it when we get real enough to question, doubt and search out our souls.

I said, "I don't know. A lot of what we have been told is hog wash."

As to hog wash, I would like to dispense with anything that does not feel like love or separates me or makes me feel superior in any way to any other person in the human family.

And please, there is no need to speak of a narrowly defined idea of spirituality or of the Bible in an effort to defend a personally held position.

For me, there are ways I choose to live when it comes to spirituality but I hold it all with open hands and I am willing to joyfully live with the questions.

"Do you think we made it all up?"

Maybe. Or maybe not.

December 30

To everything there is a season, and a time to every purpose under the heaven:

A time to be born, and a time to die; a time to plant, and a time to pluck up that which is planted;

A time to kill, and a time to heal; a time to break down, and a time to build up;

A time to weep, and a time to laugh; a time to mourn, and a time to dance;

A time to cast away stones, and a time to gather stones together; a time to embrace, and a time to refrain from embracing;

A time to get, and a time to lose; a time to keep, and a time to cast away;

A time to rend, and a time to sew; a time to keep silence, and a time to speak;

A time to love, and a time to hate; a time of war, and a time of peace.

Ecclesiastics 3: 1-8

December 31

That which is, is only grace. There is nothing more.
—Ramana Maharshi

Made in the USA
Middletown, DE
05 May 2020